The
CUBS
READER

D0769715

The CUBS READER

Edited by David Fulk and Dan Riley

REVISED EDITION

HOUGHTON MIFFLIN COMPANY

Boston • 1991

Copyright © 1991 by Dan Riley

For information about permission to reproduce selections from
this book, write to Permissions, Houghton Mifflin Company,
2 Park Street, Boston, Massachusetts 02108.

Library of Congress Cataloging-in-Publication Data
The Cubs reader / edited by David Fulk and Dan Riley. — Rev. ed.
    p.   cm.
ISBN 0-395-58779-4 (pbk.)
1. Chicago Cubs (Baseball team) 2. Chicago Cubs (Baseball team) —
History.   I. Fulk, David. II. Riley, Dan.
GV875.C6C83   1991   91-4389
796.357′64′0977311 — dc20   CIP

Printed in the United States of America

Book design by Robert Overholtzer

BTA 10 9 8 7 6 5 4 3 2 1

Grateful acknowledgment is made to the following for permission to
reprint previously published material:

"It's Been HOW Long Since the Cubs Won the World Series?" by
Sheldon Mix. Copyright © 1978, Sheldon Mix.

"Thursday, October 9, 1908" from *The Unforgettable Season* by
G. H. Fleming. Published by Holt, Rinehart and Winston. Copyright ©
1981 G. H. Fleming.

"1938: Chicago Cubs 6, Pittsburgh Pirates 5," by Gabby Hartnett as
told to Hal Totten. © *The Chicago Sun-Times.*

"The Summer of '45" (a three-part series) by David Condon.
Copyright © 1972, The Chicago Tribune Co., all rights reserved, used
with permission.

"All the Laughter Died in Sorrow," by Skip Myslenski. Copyright ©
1979, The Chicago Tribune Co., all rights reserved, used with permission.

Excerpt from "Tiger, Tiger," from *Season Ticket* by Roger Angell.
Copyright © 1988 by Roger Angell. Reprinted by permission of
Houghton Mifflin Co. (Originally appeared in *The New Yorker.*)

"One Place That Hasn't Seen the Light" by E. M. Swift. Reprinted
courtesy of *Sports Illustrated,* July 7, 1980. Copyright © 1980, Time,
Inc.

"The Battle of Wrigley Field" from *Veeck as in Wreck* by Bill Veeck with Ed Linn. Published by G. P. Putnam's Sons. Copyright © 1962 by Mary Frances Veeck and Edward Linn.

"College Haunts, 40 Years After" by David S. Broder. Copyright © 1987, *The Washington Post.*

"Let There Be Light! The Better to See Our Memories" by Joe Mantegna. Copyright © 1988 by The New York Times Co. Reprinted with permission.

"The Sun to Set on Cubs' Illusions" by Bernie Lincicome. Copyright © 1988, The Chicago Tribune Co., all rights reserved, used with permission.

"Take Me Out to a Night Game" by George F. Will. From *Newsweek,* Aug. 15, 1988. Copyright © 1988, Newsweek, Inc. All rights reserved. Reprinted by permission.

"Aweary of the Sun" by Tom Callahan. Copyright © 1988, Time Inc. Reprinted by permission.

"Mr. Hardrock, Sir" by Ira Berkow. Copyright © 1986 by The New York Times Co. Reprinted with permission.

Excerpts from *The Great American Baseball Card Flipping, Trading and Bubble Gum Book* by Brendan C. Boyd and Fred C. Harris. Copyright © 1973 by Brendan C. Boyd and Frederick C. Harris. Baseball cards copyright © Topps Chewing Gum, Inc.

"Emil the Antelope Returns" by Ira Berkow. Copyright © 1985 by The New York Times Co. Reprinted with permission.

"A Tale of Two Men and One City" by Mark Kram. Copyright © 1969. Reprinted courtesy of *Sports Illustrated,* September 29, 1969. Copyright © 1969, Time, Inc.

"Billy Williams Is In: That's What Really Counts This Week" by Raymond Coffey. Copyright © 1987, The Chicago Tribune Co., all rights reserved, used with permission.

"He Throws a Wild Card into Game" by Mike Downey. Copyright © 1989, Los Angeles Times Syndicate. Reprinted by permission.

"On Being a Cub Fan" from *The Game Is Never Over: An Appreciative History of the Chicago Cubs* by Jim Langford. Copyright © 1982 by B&L Publishing.

"The Chicago Cubs, Overdue," from *The Pursuit of Happiness and Other Sobering Thoughts* by George F. Will. Copyright © 1974 by George F. Will.

"A Visit to Wrigley — Where Hope Springs Infernal" by Harry Stein. Copyright © 1983 by Harry Stein.

"We All Had a Ball" by Roy Blount, Jr. Copyright © 1983 by Roy Blount, Jr. Reprinted by permission of International Creative Management.

"The Long-Suffering Now Insufferable" by Bernie Lincicome. Copyright © 1984, The Chicago Tribune Co., all rights reserved, used with permission.

"Opening Day, April 1987" from *Bleachers: A Summer in Wrigley Field* by Lonnie Wheeler. Published by Contemporary Books, Inc. Copyright © 1987 by Lonnie Wheeler.

Excerpt from *Bleacher Bums*. Copyright © 1977 by The Bleacher Bums Company. All inquiries regarding production should be directed to The Bleacher Bums Company, 13500 Crewe St., Van Nuys, CA 91405.

"Funny How You Can Date a Life with Baseball" by Gordon Edes. Copyright © 1984, Los Angeles Times. Reprinted by permission. (Lyrics for "A Dying Cub Fan's Last Request" by Steve Goodman, copyright © 1981, Bug Music.)

"In the End, the Cubs Are Still the Cubs" by Mike Downey. Copyright © 1989, Los Angeles Times Syndicate. Reprinted by permission.

"Would Chicago Be Losing Something If the Cubs Actually Won?" by Jon Margolis. Copyright © 1989, The Chicago Tribune Co., all rights reserved, used with permission.

Contents

THE OLD DAYS
(Good and Otherwise)

THE FRIENDLY CONFINES

DRAMATIS PERSONAE

Acknowledgments

This book would not have been possible without the cooperation and support of a good many people, some of whom are not Cub fans but are hereby forgiven that indiscretion. My particular thanks to the writers, first and foremost, whose outstanding writing made this book possible; the publications and individual copyright holders for kindly granting us permission to reprint each of the articles; Cub fans everywhere, for being and caring; and my parents, particularly my mother, who, though not a baseball fan herself, perceived the incipient Cubophilia in her young son and fed his habit by personally escorting him on many an afternoon jaunt to Wrigley Field.

Finally, I would like to thank each and every Chicago Cub, past and present, for giving their all, even in the bleakest of times, and providing more enjoyment for more people than seems decent.

D.F.

Introduction

The conversation started innocently enough.

"Hello."

"Dave! How're you doing? It's Ralph."

"Hey, Ralph."

"Long time no see, buddy. What have you been up to?"

"Oh, this and that. Actually, I've been working on a book."

"A book? You writing the Great American Novel?"

"I'm not writing, I'm editing. *The Cubs Reader,* it's a collection of some of the best writing ever done on the Cubs."

There was a pause on the line. It was one of those pauses where you know the conversation is about to take a turn for the ugly.

"Why?"

"Why? Because I'm a fan of good writing, and I'm a fan of the Cubs. Seemed like a logical project for me."

"Yeah, Dave, but . . . why?"

"What do you mean?"

"Come on, guy. Couldn't you have found a more dignified subject for your book, like 'The Changing Face of Europe' or 'The Race for the Superconductor'? Why would you want to associate your name with a bunch of losers like the Cubs?"

"What are you talking about, losers? They just won their division for the second time in six years."

"And lost the playoffs. That makes, what, forty-eight years now without a pennant?"

"Forty-four. Look, who appointed you judge, jury, and executioner on my choice of projects, anyway?"

"Hey, buddy. I'm just trying to help you preserve your good name, that's all."

Now, Ralph is not really a bad person. In fact, we'd had some great times together back in our college-chum days. But since then he'd made two life choices that led me to have serious doubts about his character: (1) he'd become a lawyer, and (2) he'd become a Mets fan. So I knew I'd have to perform my grim duty and set him straight.

"Ralph, tell me something. You're a Democrat, right?"

"Yeah. So?"

"So, how many presidential elections have the Democrats won in the last twenty-five years?"

"Dave, I know what you're getting at —"

"One, Ralph. And if you look at Jimmy Carter's record, it was the political equivalent of winning the division and losing the playoffs. But I haven't noticed you switching parties so you could be with a winner."

"Wait a minute, you're talking apples and oranges. I happen to support the Democrats on moral principle."

"Has it occurred to you that my supporting the Cubs is also a matter of moral principle?"

"Huh?"

"Tell me something else. Do you like women?"

"What do you mean? I love women. You know nobody loves women more than I do."

"Really? Even after two divorces?"

"Hey, no fair. Those were bad luck. Anyway, it so happens I'm engaged again, and this time it's gonna work out great."

"Aha! Did you hear that? Listen to yourself, Ralph. You're talking just like a Cub fan."

"Now wait a second here —"

"No, don't deny it. Face it, you're no different from me. Everybody has their own psychological equivalent of the Cubs. It's part of the human condition. I just happen to have the real thing, and you have surrogates. So don't give me this New York–superior business about besmirching my good name."

"Why are you getting so upset? All I meant was —"

"I can't discuss it anymore right now, Ralph. Just take some time and think about it. If you'll excuse me, I've got a book to edit."

All right, so maybe I was a little hard on him. I have to admit, though, there's a certain satisfaction in heaping invective on infidels like Ralph, even if they never do quite seem to get the message. Because in point of fact, there really is a kind of moral and spiritual — well, *nobility* to being a Cub fan. It's a way of saying to the world, "Hey, you arrogant so-and-so's, you can keep us out of the winner's circle, you can be snide and sarcastic, and you can make your tired jokes about us. But you can't stop us from having fun!" Which, when you get right down to it, is the whole point. And what other team can claim to have provided more fun for its devotees over the years than the Cubs? So take that, Cardinalsmetsexpospiratesphillies Fans!

Ralph and his ilk don't really understand any of this, nor could they be expected to. But they're probably a lost cause anyway, so who cares? Those of you who are reading this book, which is to say you noble masses of true believers out there, you know what I'm talking about. So do the twenty-six writers featured here, each of whom has deftly illuminated one or more of the myriad aspects of the Cub Experience. In truth, we all owe these gifted wordsmiths and their colleagues more than many of us may realize, for if there had been no outstanding writing on the Cubs, would we be nearly as powerfully aware — not to mention proud — of what an outstanding thing we've got going here? If fun really is what it's all about, then the writers of Cub-land have to be given their due for providing a hefty helping of it; and I hope and trust that, with this particular collection of factual, spiritual, whimsical, elegant, and heartfelt essays, the customary good time will be had by all.

Happy reading!

                                                                                                    D.F.

Introduction to the Revised Edition

The Cubs did not make it to the 1990 World Series of course.

But as that Series was drawing to its incredible conclusion with the Cincinnati Reds defying 30–1 odds to sweep the seemingly invincible Oakland A's, 4 games to none, the Cubs Factor finally came out of the baseball closet. Until it went mainstream during one of the CBS broadcasts of the Series, the Cubs Factor had been acknowledged only on the fringes of the game by palm readers, channelers, and people who listen to too much New Age music. But with the stunning upset of the A's by the Reds staring the baseball world in the face, the Cubs Factor could no longer be ignored as the babbling of a few far-out zanies. The outcome had confounded the geniuses who had taken every ordinary means at their command in evaluating the competitors.

Old-time reporters who'd seen each of the teams at least once on a game of the week — or who had at least read about them in *TV Guide* — offered their usual seat-of-the-pants position-by-position analyses of the teams. And the A's were superior.

The sabermetricians broke out their slide rules and measuring cups. And the A's were still superior.

And the boys at the Elias Sports Bureau processed a whole lot of data on which team had the most guys who got the most hits with the most other guys on in pressure situations. And sure enough, the A's won there, too.

But the A's didn't win on the field, and the only way anyone could — well, rationally — account for it was the Cubs
Factor — which is, in case you missed it, based on the
startling statistic that the team with the most ex-Cubbies on
its Series roster has lost every World Series since 1945, the
last year the Cubs themselves were in the Fall Classic.

If this continues, we can easily envision pennant contenders annually purging themselves of ex-Cubbies before
their postseason rosters are frozen. This phenomenon is too
new, of course, and frankly too incendiary, to be treated in
this revised edition of *The Cubs Reader*. Besides, as the
pages ahead reveal, the Cubs have had enough troubles of
their own coping with rosters full of future ex-Cubbies.

D.R.

THE OLD DAYS
(Good and Otherwise)

Cub fans under age fifty may find it hard to fathom, but there was a time when the Cubs were not thought of as perennial doormats. In fact, if you go back far enough, they were actually the scourge of the National League. They carried their reputation much as the Bears do today: as big, tough, colorful customers from a big, tough, colorful city. Latter-day cynics need to be reminded that, if you look at things in a historical context — and when should you not? — the Cubs' record stands up just fine against that of every other major league team (excepting, if you must, the Yankees). So we begin with a few glimpses into the Cubs' storied and occasionally glorious past.

First we time-warp back to 1908, the days of Three-Finger Brown, Big Ed Reulbach, Tinker-to-Evers-to-Chance — and the Cubs' last world championship. Sheldon Mix recounts the '08 Cubs' exploits against the backdrop of a world that seems as removed from today's as the reign of King Tut. Then G. H. Fleming offers a collection of newspaper accounts on the end of the crazy 1908 pennant race. The Bruins collected three pennants during the '30s, but, as the piece by Gabby Hartnett attests, they were more successful at generating memorable moments than bringing home world championships. Of course, we've all been reminded ad nauseam of the significance of 1945, but David Condon's spirited account of that season should temporarily douse the pain and rekindle the pride in Cub fans' bosoms. Next, Skip Myslenski recalls the summer of

'69 — the Year of Infamy, a black hole of anguish in our collective Cubophiliac souls. Finally, Roger Angell reports on the fateful Cubs–Padres series of '84, pausing along the way to ponder the unique status of the North Siders and their devotees in baseball history.

Sheldon Mix

It's Been HOW Long
Since the Cubs
Won the World Series?

The year was 1908, and if baseball fans anywhere but Chicago were crying "break up the Cubs," it was understandable. In that year, the West Siders (they hadn't moved north to Wrigley Field yet) won their third straight National League championship and their second consecutive World Series — the last the Cubs have won. (In fact, in the 11 seasons beginning with 1903, the team won four NL titles, never finishing lower than third.)

It was a far different time for everybody, not just for Cub fans. The Republicans, for example, had majorities in both House and Senate, and in New York it was against the law for a woman to smoke in public. It was a time of chaperones and front porches and chautauquas, when "Shine On, Harvest Moon" was a new number. Cuspidors, or spittoons, were familiar accessories in offices and stores, in hotel lobbies, even in parlors, and some men were skilled at hitting them from a good distance away.

Theodore Roosevelt was President — a strong one — and a striking, lusty personality. His choice word for expressing enthusiastic approval was "Bully!" and he had a particular fondness for the West African proverb, "Speak softly and carry a big stick; you will go far."

More than half of Americans lived on farms or in towns with fewer than 2,500 inhabitants, but between 1900 and 1910 the rural population increased by only 11 percent while the urban population rose by about 40 percent. Only one out of 10 houses in 1908 was wired for electricity.

How long ago was 1908? The University of Chicago was football champion of the Big 10.

When the Cubs last won the World Series, the late Philip K. Wrigley was a 13-year-old pupil at Chicago Latin School. Another decade would pass before his father, William Jr., took over as majority stockholder of the Cubs. The team's home during its world-championship years was a shabby old ball park at Polk and Wolcott, where County Hospital now stands. Best-known Cubs of that era were the double-play threesome: short-stop Joe Tinker, second baseman Johnny Evers, and manager-first baseman Frank Chance. They were immortalized when a celebrated fan of the New York Giants, Franklin P. Adams, wrote this poem in his newspaper column:

> These are the saddest of possible words:
> Tinker to Evers to Chance.
> Trio of bear Cubs fleeter than birds,
> Tinker to Evers to Chance.
> Ruthlessly pricking our gonfallon bubble,
> Making a Giant hit into a double —
> Words that are heavy with nothing but trouble:
> Tinker to Evers to Chance.

It was the Edwardian Age, with its newly made fortunes, lavish entertaining, private railway cars, eight-course meals, and big waistlines. Names like Carnegie, Vanderbilt, Gould, Harriman, Rockefeller, and Morgan were mighty in the land.

Oklahoma had been admitted to the Union in 1907 as the 46th state, and trans-Atlantic wireless service began between Ireland and Nova Scotia. Nearly a million immigrants came to the United States in each of the 14 years following 1900; the peak was in 1907, with 1,285,349. On Sept. 12 of that year the *Lusitania,* largest steamship in the world, docked in New

York on her maiden voyage. Two months later she set a record by crossing the Atlantic in 4 days, 18 hours, 40 minutes.

The United States, having defeated Spain in 1898, was getting its initial taste of world power. Teddy Roosevelt was eager to see dirt fly at the Panama Canal project, where construction had been inching along since 1904. So in 1907 he turned over the job to the Army Corps of Engineers and put 49-year-old Lt. Col. George Washington Goethals in charge of construction. He picked the right man. An associate on the project said of Goethals, "The only time the colonel isn't working is from 10 p.m. to 6 a.m., when he's asleep." (The first ship passed through the canal in January, 1914, after numerous obstacles — including some 140 million cubic yards of earth — had been dealt with.)

Baseball quizzes often ask who played third base in the legendary Tinker-Evers-Chance infield. Answer: an under-rated veteran named Harry Steinfeldt, acquired from Cincin-nati in time for the 1906 season. Others on the pennant-winners of 1906–07–08: Johnny Kling was first-string catcher, and the outfield had strong-armed Jimmy Sheckard in left, Jimmy Slagle in center, and Frank "Wildfire" Schulte in right. Most memorable of the pitchers was Mordecai "Three-Fingered" Brown, a 20-game winner six straight years. His hurling col-leagues included Ed Reulbach, Orval Overall, and John "Jack the Giant Killer" Pfiester. Of 322 games the Cubs won in 1906–07–08, those four were the winners of 235.

By 1907, Great Britain, France, and Russia had arranged to become allies. On the other side of Europe's scene was the Triple Alliance of Germany, Austria-Hungary, and Italy. At the Second International Peace Conference at The Hague, there was talk but no practical action on disarmament or limitation of warfare's methods. An American plea for a court of international justice was voted down.

Mainly to impress Japan's jingoists with American naval power and readiness for trouble, Roosevelt wanted to send the United States fleet, second largest in the world, on a cruise around the globe. Congress balked at supplying money for the venture, partly because of the cost, partly out of fear that the Japanese might attack the fleet without warning. Aroused, the President said there was enough money to get the ships to the Pacific, where they would remain until Congress had a change of heart. He got his way. "The Great White Fleet" steamed out of Hampton Roads, Va., on Dec. 16, 1907.

In 1908, wage-earners worked about 10 hours daily, six days a week. The American Federation of Labor, whose ranks in 1898 had numbered 278,000, was pushing toward 2 million members. A survey of working women indicated that only those in the professions were earning the $500 a year considered necessary for a decent standard of living. The following year, the Supreme Court upheld an Oregon law limiting women's daily working hours to 10. Black intellectuals, led by William E. B. DuBois, were meeting annually at Niagara Falls, Ontario, to discuss racial advancement and to formulate demands. This would lead in 1909 to the birth of the National Association for the Advancement of Colored People.

Dress was severe and formal. Men's suits were heavy the year-round and generally dark. In the countryside during high-temperature months they might wear white flannels or white ducks, but there were no summer-weight suits. Collars were high, stiff, often detachable. Cuffs also were stiff and detachable. Well-to-do women wore silk stockings; those with less money in their purses made do with black or white cotton hose — not that it could have made much difference to the girl-watchers, because even when playing golf or tennis, a woman was expected to wear a skirt reaching within two or three inches of the ground. The shirtwaist was considered daring in 1907 when, as the "peek-a-boo," it had tiny perforations embroidered at its edges. Even in hot weather, women customarily wore layers and layers of underclothes, notably a whalebone corset designed to force the female form into an hourglass shape.

After winning 116 games in 1906 — a major league record that still stands — the Cubs were rock-solid favorites to beat their South Side rivals, the White Sox, in the World Series. The Sox had won the American League pennant that year despite an anemic team batting average of .228 that earned them the nickname "Hitless Wonders." The Cub players were so confident that before the opening game they discussed what kind of prize they'd choose after dispensing with the formality of beating the White Sox. But the "Hitless Wonders," refusing to be awed, calmly captured the Series 4 games to 2. A year later the Cubs' World Series opponent was Detroit, led at the plate by Ty Cobb and "Wahoo" Sam Crawford. Some quarters predicted that "Cobb alone will beat the Cubs." Eager to offset the embarrassment of the previous October, the Cubs sized up the Tigers perfectly and scored a four-game sweep after the first contest ended in a tie. Crawford could hit no better than .238 against the Cubs. Cobb, the American League batting champion, was held to .200.

Eager to live like princes, American millionaires preferred foreign styles, foreign furnishings, foreign cars, foreign works of art. They also wanted international marriages for their daughters. One of Charles Dana Gibson's satirical drawings from the period shows a foreigner whose sole asset is his title, but he's the one whom the millionaire's wife wants her daughter to wed. By the end of 1903, McCall's magazine was able to list 57 international marriages. Why the fondness for such alliances? A noble wedding, wealthy parents felt, provided the authentic stamp of aristocracy at the apex of the social pyramid. One such glittering marriage in 1908 united Gladys Vanderbilt with Count Laszlo Szechenyi, a Hungarian, thus transforming the daughter of Cornelius II into a countess.

Chicago had eight newspapers in 1908, and their stories chronicled the actions of the city's mayor, Fred A. Busse, and the triumphs of Chicago's golf champion, Chick Evans, who as an Evanston Academy student had recently won the Western Interscholastic Golf Championship. Sportswriters found good copy in the University of Chicago's football coach, Amos Alonzo Stagg, whose innovations included the huddle, shift, man-in-motion, and end-around play, and whose Maroons beat Purdue 39–0 and Minnesota 29–0 on their way to the Big 10 title. The heaviest man on that championship squad weighed 195 pounds; the pair of guards weighed 163 and 165.

Newspaper ads offered a pound of pure epsom salts for 3 cents, a quart of witch hazel for 23 cents, union suits priced from $1 to $3, a piano in a mahogany case for $110. Marshall Field & Co. advertised petticoats "of fine rustling taffeta silk, in black and colors, made with deep sectional ruffle, trimmed with narrow bias bands," all for $3.95. It cost 10 cents to enter Riverview Amusement Park, a dollar to make a round trip between Chicago and St. Joseph–Benton Harbor on a Graham & Morton excursion steamer, 25 or 50 cents to see *Charley's Aunt* at the Great Northern. There were 337 theatrical touring companies in 1908. Chicago's shows that year starred Denis O'Sullivan in *Peggy Machree* at the McVicker's, Fritzi Scheff in Victor Herbert's *The Prima Donna* at the Studebaker, and Raymond Hitchcock in *The Merry-Go-Round* at the Chicago Opera House. Among the artists performing at Orchestra Hall were Paderewski, Walter Damrosch, Fritz Kreisler, and Rudolph Ganz.

Songs that went to the top of their class in popularity 70 years ago included "Cuddle Up a Little Closer," "The Yama Yama Man," and "Up in a Balloon" (Chicago hosted the International Balloon Races that year). Another new hit was "Take Me Out to the Ball Game," which quickly became baseball's national anthem. But it would be 20 years before the song's composer, Albert von Tilzer, took himself out to see his first ball game.

The Cubs, Giants, and Pirates were locked in close battle for the National League pennant as the 1908 season came down to its final weeks. On Sept. 23 the Cubs and Giants were tied 1–1 in the ninth inning at the Polo Grounds. The Giants were batting with two outs. With Moose McCormick on third and Fred Merkle on first, Al Bridwell lined a single to center. As

McCormick came home with what appeared to be the winning run, jubilant fans ran onto the field. Seeing McCormick cross the plate, Merkle didn't bother to run all the way to second but stopped a few feet short and then headed toward the clubhouse with his teammates; a new player, only 19 years old, he had seen other baserunners do the same in similar circumstances. But Johnny Evers, the Cubs' alert and hotly competitive second baseman — they called him "the Crab" — wasn't the type to shrug his shoulders at such casualness. He started howling for the ball. As for what took place next, there is considerable disagreement.

Evers always maintained that the ball was thrown to him and that he stepped on second, forcing Merkle and nullifying McCormick's run, that umpire Hank O'Day watched him make the play and told him that the Giants' run didn't count. The Giants disputed all this, saying that "Iron Man" Joe McGinnity had got the ball and tossed it into the crowd. The case quickly landed in the lap of the league president, who ruled that the game ended in a tie and that, if necessary to the outcome of the pennant race, would have to be replayed. The Giants protested the decision but lost.

After eliminating the Pirates on the last Sunday of the season, the Cubs ended the season in a tie with the Giants, who swept their final series with Boston. The replay was set for Oct. 8 in New York. On the big day an overflow crowd tore down part of the fence and was about to overrun the field until police enforced order with the aid of a fire hose. Hungry for victory over the hated Cubs (and there was reciprocity: "If you didn't honestly and furiously hate the Giants, you weren't a real Cub," said Joe Tinker), Giant fans hurled bottles, cushions, and vocal abuse at the Chicagoans, but it was not to be their heroes' day: Solving the brilliant Christy Mathewson (he won 37 games that season) for four runs in the third inning, the Cubs won, 4 to 2. A third consecutive pennant was theirs.

The automobile was gearing up to push the horse out to pasture. In 1895 there were four autos registered in the U.S.; in 1900, about 8,000. By 1908 the total had risen to 194,400.

General Motors was incorporated that year, and Henry Ford introduced his Model T. Previously, cars were seen mostly in cities and around fashionable resorts and were viewed mainly as playthings for the rich. In 1906 Princeton president Woodrow Wilson had said, "Nothing has spread socialistic feeling in this country more than the use of the automobile," adding: "To the countryman they (automobiles) are a picture of arrogance and wealth, with all its independence and carelessness." Seven years later he became the first president to ride to an inauguration in an automobile; the make chosen for the occasion was a Rolls-Royce.

People were singing "In My Merry Oldsmobile" in 1908, but they were likely to be talking about the 4-cylinder, 10-horsepower Model T Ford. The light, economical "Tin Lizzie" caught the public's fancy, and soon the Ford factory couldn't keep up with the demand. The price of that first Model T was $850, but by 1917 it was lowered to $360. Ford was able to produce inexpensive cars by concentrating on a single model and pioneering in production techniques.

Signs of the fast-approaching automotive age were everywhere in 1908 — on Michigan Avenue south of 14th Street, for example, where 400 candle-power gas arcs lit Chicago's "automobile row." There was much ballyhoo over a New York–to–Paris auto race, won by an American car that covered the course in five and a half months. Some Pennsylvanians made the first family auto trip across the U.S., leaving Los Angeles on April 24, arriving in New York on May 26.

The first steel-and-glass building was erected that year in Berlin. Frank Lloyd Wright designed for Frederick Robie on Chicago's South Side what may be his most famous "prairie house." And it was in 1908 that Daniel H. Burnham unveiled his plan for Chicago, urging the city's leaders to "Make no little plans. They have no magic to stir men's blood. Make big plans. Aim high in hope and work, remembering that a noble, logical diagram once recorded will never die. . . ."

Who were the newborn in 1908? Lyndon Johnson and Nelson Rockefeller, Herbert Von Karajan, Henri Cartier-

Bresson, Edward R. Murrow, William Saroyan, and Alistair Cooke. Also some infants born in time for Hollywood's hey-day: Joan Crawford, Bette Davis, Paul Henreid, Fred Mac-Murray, Jimmy Stewart, Don Ameche, Milton Berle, Ray Milland, Burgess Meredith, Greer Garson, Rex Harrison, and Lou Costello. Rimsky-Korsakov died that summer. So did Grover Cleveland. Grover Cleveland Alexander's pitching debut in pro ball was two years away. Babe Ruth could be reached at St. Mary's Industrial School in Baltimore, and Ernest Hemingway was a 4th-grader in Oak Park. Sinclair Lewis, who would become the first American to win the Nobel Prize for Literature, was not long out of Yale. Ring Lardner joined the sports department of *The Tribune* in time for the World Series.

Teddy Roosevelt's choice as his successor in the White House, William Howard Taft, sent William Jennings Bryan to his third defeat in November. A genial 350-pounder, Taft was the first President to play golf and the President who initiated the custom of throwing out the first ball of the major league season. He wielded a big stick against the trusts: In his four years in office he brought 65 indictments under the Sherman Anti-Trust Act, as opposed to Roosevelt's 44 in nearly eight years as President. Taft also took the first steps toward an income tax by proposing a constitutional amendment that Congress passed and the states ratified with little opposition. When the tax was first imposed, in 1913, a married man whose net income was $10,000 paid about $60; one with a $20,000 net income owed the government about $160.

If Americans weren't yet weeping over the income tax in 1908, many were shedding tears over the year's top best-seller, *The Trail of the Lonesome Pine.* Mystery fans were reading Mary Roberts Rinehart's newest, *The Circular Stair-case.* Gertrude Stein published her *Three Lives,* Arnold Bennett his *Old Wives' Tale.* It was the year of Kenneth Grahame's *The Wind in the Willows,* G. K. Chesterton's *The Man Who Was Thursday,* E. M. Forster's *A Room with a View.*

On State Street a man visiting a bird-and-animal store (they

weren't called pet shops then) was bitten by a bear cub —
not long before the Detroit Tigers were chased off the
diamond by a pack of Cubs.

*The Detroit Tigers repeated as American League champions
in 1908, and in the World Series lost again to Chicago, this
time 4 games to 1. The Cubs thus became the first team to win
the Series two years in a row. In Chicago, awaiting news of the
deciding game, played in Detroit on Oct. 14, was an inveterate
baseball fan named George M. Cohan, then playing at the
Colonial Theater in* The Yankee Prince. *Two nights later,
Cohan left his dressing room after the performance and hurried
to Rector's restaurant, where he hosted the victorious Cubs and
their wives at an evening of wining, dining, and toasting.*

*For the Cubs and their fans at that moment, success in the
World Series must have seemed a laurel easily grasped, suggest-
ing a future with more of the same. Yet the next 69 Octobers on
the North Side (including the pennant years of 1910, 1918,
1929, 1932, 1935, 1938, and 1945) would pass without producing another such cause for celebration. How many more will
pass?*

G. H. Fleming

Thursday, October 9, 1908

Editor's Note: The following newspaper accounts of the end of the 1908 pennant race were assembled by G. H. Fleming for his book *The Unforgettable Season*. We've left these accounts just the way they appeared in New York and Chicago papers of the day as evidence that though the Cubs may not play as well as they used to, folks sure do write better.

On October 8, in New York, the Chicago Cubs won the National League championship of 1908 by beating the Giants 4 to 2. Winning pitcher, Brown; losing pitcher, Mathewson.

One terrible inning brought the Giants the sting of final defeat after a season of glorious struggling in the face of every possible discouragement and handicap. Fighting for a pennant already won, as far as baseball on the field is concerned, it was the fate of McGraw's gallant band to lose the crucial struggle through the wavering for a moment of the great pitcher whose splendid skill and still more splendid courage have done so much to make this the most wonderful fight the game of baseball has ever known.

It lacked 15 minutes of 3 o'clock when Klem called play in the struggle on which the attention of the whole nation was centered. As warm as on a perfect August day, with a blue sky above, conditions could not have been more perfect. Fifty thousand pairs of eyes were focused on the field where

the tense gray players of Chicago, fighting to lead the league
for the third time, awaited the issue, and fifty times that many
gazed at bulletin boards, at tickers, at electric boards that
showed every play, and at other countless devices waiting all
over the country to carry the instant word of the fight from
the living, throbbing wires that began at the ends of nervous
fingers in the press box.

Sheckard faced "Matty" for the first ball of the game, and a
great sigh — the tension was too great for a cheer — went
up as Klem's raised hand flashed a strike. A moment later
tense tongues loosed in a mighty roar as Sheckard swung
wildly at a slow, floating ball and went back to the bend. Two
strikes were quickly called on Evers, and then he shot a
bounding hit to Herzog, which was thrown to Tenney for the
second out. Schulte was the next man, and Mathewson,
exulting in his strength, struck him out.

It was a superb start, and when the first ball that Pfiester
pitched hit Tenney on the arm a great roar of joy filled the air.
Herzog walked on four balls, and the crowd fairly shrieked at
Bresnahan for a hit. But the third strike fooled the great
catcher completely, and Herzog, foolishly dancing off first
base, was thrown out by the deadly arm of Kling, completing
a play that may have cost the game. Donlin was next up, and
when he smashed the ball down the right field foul line for two
bases the crowd was lost in such transports of joy as Tenney
scored that it could hardly take the time to hoot Chance for
shrieking that the ball was a foul.

Then came a base on balls to Seymour, and after a long
conference Chance sent for Brown, and Pfiester walked sadly
to the bench. The crowd went wild with joy, but its rapture
was short-lived, as the three-fingered pitcher ended the inning
and a great chance to break up the game by striking Devlin
out.

Chance whipped a single to left to start the next inning, but
a lightning throw by Matty caught the Chicago manager off
first base, and the roar from Chance on the decision seemed
likely for a moment to break up the game. He argued with
Johnstone for five minutes, and the umpire threatened twice

to put him off the field — which he would have been justified
in doing. Chance came back wringing his hands, and Hofman,
waiting his turn at bat, threw his bat on the ground. He had
said nothing, but his act was evidently thought more serious
than his manager's unless it is that Klem is made of sterner
stuff than Johnstone, for the doughty umpire behind the bat
ordered Chicago's center fielder off the grounds. Then Steinfeldt and Howard, who had replaced Hofman, struck out.

Schulte helped Brown in the second inning by two fine
catches in right field, the second, of a hard drive by Bridwell,
being a really great play. Tinker gave more help by a fine stop
of Matty's hard grounder, and all was ready for the tragedy
that was to turn wild joy and rosy hopes into gloom.

Here was Tinker, swinging the mighty bat that had so often
made trouble for Mathewson, and once more he swung it
with fatal effect. Matty had looked around as he prepared to
pitch, and waved his fielders back, but Seymour had paid no
heed, and as Tinker smashed the ball far away to left center,
Seymour saw his fatal error even as he raced back. He made
a great leap for the ball, but just missed a catch that would
have been easy had he been ten feet further back.

Tinker was safe on third when the ball came back and
almost walked home when Kling singled viciously to left.
Brown sacrificed, and Sheckard raised a fly that Seymour
caught, being where he belonged this time. On such small
things do great issues hang. Had Seymour been ten feet
further back and taken Tinker's fly, the inning, and the game,
would have ended with Sheckard's fly, without a score. But,
as it was, there was still a man to be put out, and before he
had been retired, Evers had walked and Schulte and Chance
had doubled, sending in three more runs and winning the
game, as it turned out.

Gloom was in the crowd everywhere, but not on the New
York bench. Matty had been hit hard, but McGraw refused to
take him out, and his confidence was fully justified in the four
innings Matty was still to pitch.

The Giants tried too hard to come back in their third inning.
Tenney began with a clean single, the first hit off Brown, and

after Herzog had fouled to Kling, Bresnahan planted the ball into right field for another safety. But Donlin could only force Bresnahan at second, and Seymour sent a groan through the crowd with a fly to Sheckard.

Then it was a procession to and from the bat until the sixth inning, when both nines were active. Chance drove out his third hit — he was the only man on either side with more than one hit — but Bresnahan caught him stealing with a perfect throw to Herzog. Steinfeldt also singled, but Howard struck out again.

Agony was piled on agony when New York came up for the seventh time. With the crowd shrieking for the "lucky" seventh to work its spell, Devlin faced Brown and drove out as pretty a single as was ever made. McCormick followed with another safe drive, and when Bridwell walked, filling the bases, with none out, an explosion of dynamite would not have been heard.

Mathewson was the next man up, and the crowd groaned when McGraw sent Doyle to bat for him. It was strange that he should do so, for Matty is a strong batter, and Doyle has not faced an opposing pitcher in a big game since he was hurt weeks ago. Doyle hit a high foul that fell into Kling's hands. Tenney sent a run home with a long sacrifice fly, but two men were left on base when Tinker threw Herzog out and New York's best chance was gone.

Wiltse finished the game, and only a great play by McCormick saved a run in the eighth. Evers had doubled with one out and gone to third when Tenney's error left Schulte safe at first base. Chance drove a fly to McCormick, and after a great catch, McCormick made a superb throw to the plate that enabled Bresnahan to put Evers out.

New York could do nothing in the last two innings, and four pitched balls in the ninth disposed of Devlin, McCormick, and Bridwell. Chicago had won the game and the pennant.

— New York Tribune

NEW YORK, OCT. 8 — All honor will be given the Cubs as long as baseball is played, for what they did this afternoon in the shadow of Coogan's Bluff. They won not only decisively but cleanly and gamely, while their adversaries attempted to take cheap and tricky advantage of them in every way. The world's champions were compelled even to fight for the privilege of getting the meager practice allowed by the rules before the game.

Nor was defeat and loss of the pennant New York's only disgrace, for the crowd contained at least one man who will be remembered to Gotham's discredit as long as Merkle. That is the dastard who sneaked up behind Manager Chance as the Cubs were leaving the scene of victory and struck him a blow in the neck.

Before the Cub manager could wheel to defend himself the coward had been swallowed up in the tremendous throng. A hurried examination of the manager at the dressing room by a surgeon in attendance disclosed the assailant probably had broken a cartilage in Chance's neck but it was not expected that the injury would keep him out of the world's series battles.

To Mordecai Brown will belong the lion's share of credit for Chicago's third pennant — to Mordecai and Joe Tinker. It was the mighty three-fingered star who pitched both of the crucial and "final" games of the year. It was the fleet-footed and scrappy shortstop who led the Cubs in that terrific unbeatable assault in the third inning which nailed the game to Chicago's flagpole and broke the back of the great Mathewson.

The game was preceded by a bit of petty trickery by the Giants which probably had much to do with prompting the cowardly slugging which was handed Manager Chance at the close.

The crowd was so great it compelled locking the gates long before time to start the game, and it was decided not to wait until 3 o'clock, as everybody who could get inside was already there.

But the 15 minutes gained in time was taken out of the Cubs' practice. The Giants took their full allotment of 20 minutes for batting practice, then when the Cubs started on their practice they were stopped at the end of five minutes. Chance objected to this after his club had traveled 1,000 miles and had no other opportunity to limber up. As McGinnity stepped to the plate under orders to begin knocking grounders to the Giants for fielding practice Chance tried to brush him away, and the "Iron Man" raised his bat threateningly.

For an instant it looked the beginning of a riot, which would forever have disgraced the game, but other players of both teams rushed in and surrounded the belligerents, smoothing out the incident quickly. When the thing was explained to Chance there was nothing for him to do but smile contemptuously at the trick and acquiesce. The Cubs proved later they didn't need the other 15 minutes of batting practice.

— I. E. Sanborn, *Chicago Tribune*

If we turn the clock back to about an hour or two before the game begins we note that some of the boxes still remain vacant. This is because the ticket holders are in the street trying vainly to get inside. But up there in her usual place leaning over the rail is little Mabel Hite, wife of Mike Donlin.

Everybody is happy and hopeful, for the game hasn't begun yet, and it is frequently stated and never disputed that this is the limit for baseball enthusiasm. It's also the greatest ever, outer sight or big casino, according to who is telling you. And if you listen to Clayton Hamilton, who writes books to which Brander Matthews, the greatest Simple Speller in captivity, writes introductions, you learn that the Polo Grounds are "really the thematic centre of the cosmic scheme," whatever that may be. All this time everybody and everything is getting cheered and pelted with wads of newspaper.

A fat man comes into the right-field bleachers carrying a baby who may yet grow up to be a pitcher like Matty. He is cheered frantically and he grabs the kid with one hand and waves at the crowd with the other. Pretty girls are cheered, homely girls are cheered, fat men, thin men, tall men, short men, the girl with a hat as big as three of Fred Tenney's mitts — anything and everything for a cheer.

Now a couple of players reserved from the minor leagues appear from the clubhouse and begin to throw the ball around the diamond that has only recently been uncovered. Uncovered from what? Why, from the huge canvas sheets that have been spread on it all night. They put the diamond to bed early the night before so that it would get a good night's rest for the game of all games.

Smiling Larry Doyle, who was the Giants' regular second baseman until he hurt his leg a month ago, is the first of the regulars to show. He gets many cheers.

And then from the clubhouse emerges a melancholy figure. Shall we say it is the figure of the man who lost the pennant? Well, anyhow, it's the figure of Fred Merkle, and everybody knows that if he'd run to second when Bridwell made that safe hit at the end of the now famous disputed game the pennant would be waving from the flagstaff in center field. Amid a silence that cuts, Merkle crosses the field and begins to toss a ball about. It's clear that he feels worse than anybody else about it. Nobody has the heart to jeer him. But all the same————

Suddenly several thousand persons are released from durance and allowed to scamper to standing room behind the ropes all about the field. It looks like the serpentine dance after a victory for the Blue on Yale Field. A moment ago the field was green; now it's black.

There aren't enough real cops to boss a lively Sunday school class, and how the deuce things are ever going to be straightened out doesn't appear, unless you've been there before and know that when the umpire is ready for play the field will clear itself like magic. Everybody begins to get happily restless, and one fan says to another, "Boy, you'll be able to tell your grandchildren about this day when the Cubs — or————" Fearful of the outcome he rubs his chin doubtfully and doesn't finish.

"Robber!" "Bandit!" "Quitter!" howls the crowd all at once. The row begins in the right-field bleachers and runs all over the field as Frank Chance appears from the clubhouse, loafing

carelessly along on his bowed legs and looking as if he hadn't
a care in the world. Roars, hoots, hisses, jeers are showered
on him as he advances, but he smiles pleasantly as if the
freedom of the city had been conferred on him. Just behind
him comes Three-Fingered Brown. He is also called a number
of things which he isn't. He doesn't seem to mind either.

But there's a greater uproar yet when John McGraw shows
up, accompanied by the lean and haggard Tenney, and the
New York manager has to doff his cap before the row lets up.
One by one the rest of the Giants appear.

The New Yorks take batting practice methodically, one hit
to each man. Then the Cubs go in for theirs. More roars,
more hisses, more catcalls, howls of contempt, shrieks of
"Oh, you robbers!" "You brigands!" And you think if you were
a Cub you'd hunt for the nearest cyclone cellar. But the Cubs
wallop the horsehide as cheerfully as if the stands were
empty. Meanwhile the jeers keep on. Somebody in the stands
catches a foul tip from a Cub's bat. A hundred voices shout:
"Keep it! Keep it! Don't give it back! Murphy will cry his
eyes out if you keep it."

Meantime the twirlers are warming up, Pfiester, the left-
hander, for the Cubs, and the only Matty for the Giants. This
doesn't take long and at a quarter of three o'clock the real
trouble begins. It is time.

— New York *Sun*

Never before has the capacity of Coogan's Bluff been strained
beyond the limit as it was yesterday. Never before have veteran
hillbillies, who have worn the grass out in their accustomed
places, been rudely shoved aside by strangers and vandals occupying their favorite spots. Every hillbillie tradition was ruthlessly ripped to shreds by the pushing thousands, and Coogan's
was no longer the Coogan's of other days.

By 2 o'clock Coogan's was loaded to the gunnels and the
tens of thousands stretched along the entire semi-circle from
the Jumel Mansion to Eighth avenue. For nearly a mile there
was a mass of people lining stairs, viaducts, streets, Speed-

way, bluffs, crags, rocks, peaks, grass, plots, trees, and any other available space not previously occupied.

The view from Coogan's was gorgeous and beggared description. It was one of those perfect October days which so seldom come when you want them, and the scene was like a Turner picture. The broad bosom of the Harlem River palpitated in the Autumn glow, the hazy blue of the Bronx draped the towering palaces along the heights overlooking the silver stream, the city to the south stretched away into limitless azure, the bargains in real estate along Edgecombe avenue littered on their sacred sites, while at the foot of the bluff the eye rested on the gleaming billboards at the far end of the Polo Grounds.

If 35,000 were inside the fence, 35,000,000 were outside — the way they covered the ground and the roofs — but probably not so many as that. Never in the history of the game have there been so many to see a game who didn't see it. The standees had the call and no mistake. There were hundreds of women on the bluff, and one woman had brought her knitting along, and calmly sat on the grass and knitted while the pennant went to Chicago. She must have been a Chicago woman. Up on the lawn of the Jumel Mansion was a group of spectators. Somebody said George Washington, Aaron Burr, and Mme. Jumel were among those present. A society reporter (lady) from Brooklyn made a note of it. The enthusiasm was immense and intense, and soon soap boxes and other coigns of vantage began to appear at the back of the firing line along the bluff. Anything over two inches rented for 25 cents, and 10 cents an inch above that. Along the road, back of the bluff, delivery wagons, cabs, and automobiles lined the curb. Persons occupying them had a fine view of the backs of the front row. It was inspiring.

A little dumpy man, who couldn't see above the hip pocket of the men in front of him, said he was going home. Immediately there were cries of "Lynch him! He's a quitter!" and other personal remarks of a similar nature. He apologized and stayed till the game was over.

After a while — two hours after a while — somebody in front announced the game had begun. A hush fell on the throng on Coogan's Bluff. Every breath was baited. Never in the history of the game had there been such a moment. It sounded like a pork packer's cheer for Upton Sinclair.

— W. J. Lampton, *New York Times*

Manager Frank Chance of the Cubs was assaulted twice yesterday. As if the blow Joe McGinnity handed him before the game was not sufficient, a frenzied fan had to inflict even more serious injury on the belligerent, hustling leader of the Chicago team.

Immediately after the failure of the Giants to score in the ninth, and it was all over but the shouting for the Cubs, Chance, with Pitcher Pfiester and Catcher Kling, started for the clubhouse. The trio kept their eyes on the crowd piling out of the east end of the big stand and out of the right-field bleachers. The policemen on duty were also apprehensive and closed around Chance and his teammates.

A fan who was scarlet from excitement and wrath bowled over two cops and let loose a right-hand swing to Chance's chin. Chance threw up his head quickly and a blow caught him flush in the neck. He went down on his knees and gasped for breath. While policemen were fighting the crowd back, someone landed a stinger on Pfiester's right jaw, staggering him. Johnny Kling fought like a Trojan for his teammates and his own skin.

A horde of policemen closed in around the three Chicago players and dragged them through the crowd like a football team rushing the men with the ball over the line. The uniformed officers found their clubs ineffective against the press of the howling mob, and revolvers were drawn. This seemed to stop the rush, for the mob stood back.

Chance and his two fellow-players were literally catapulted over and through the surging, howling mob of fans. An attendant in the clubhouse threw wide the door of the press entrance and the Chicago players were thrown inside. A little policeman defended the door in Thermopylae fashion. With the mob about him and his brother policemen unable to reach him, he held that door with stones, pieces of boards and water cans hurled at him.

Manager Chance was found to have been rather badly hurt. The blow had broken a cartilage in his neck. Together with President Murphy he was hustled to an automobile and hurried away before the crowd discovered the identity of the pair.

A conference resulted in the decision that it would be best for players to leave singly or in pairs and thus avoid attention. Pitcher Pfiester wasn't much hurt by the slam he got. Mordecai Brown was one of the last to leave. As he started to walk the long chute toward the elevated railway station at 155th street, two policemen in uniform stepped up to accompany him. Brown looked at them.

"You fellows get away from me!" yelled Brown. "Those uniforms will surely tip me off." The policemen withdrew and the marvelous three-fingered one wandered unmolested in his ordinary street clothes.

A physician was summoned to the Hotel Somerset, where the Cubs put up, to examine Chance's throat. It was found that while the crushed cartilage will give the captain some pain, he will probably be all right in a day or two. Hot towels were applied to his neck and Chance said he would continue this treatment on the train en route to Detroit. Chance was sick from the blow and unable to eat dinner.

"I have no ill feeling against anyone," said Chance to a reporter at his hotel, "but I don't see why I should be picked out as a mark for folks that wish to indulge in such calisthenics. Certainly my actions today did not warrant any such treatment as I received."

— New York *American*

Two stupid plays lost the championship to the Giants. Merkle's boyish desire to be the first man in the clubhouse on Sept. 23 was the first offense. Cy Seymour's wretched fielding yesterday was in a great measure responsible for the loss of the game.

In the third inning Tinker was the first batter to face Mathewson. Tinker is a bold, bad hitter against the Giants. Seymour was playing a short field, and he stubbornly refused to budge, though Matty and Donlin both signed him to go further back.

Tinker's fly to center should have been an easy out. It would have been had Seymour played the batter properly and it would have been caught had Seymour not misjudged it so badly. Instead of sprinting back and turning around, Seymour kept taking short backward steps. Finally he lunged at the ball and missed it altogether. The fans in centerfield moaned and after the game many of them said it was a play that any schoolboy fielder would have made. Then Cyrus groped about in the crowd and fielded the ball very slowly, allowing Tinker to get to third. Had this fly been caught chances are there would have been no runs in that inning, and the opportunity for a shut-out would have been splendid.

The scene yesterday was really the most disgraceful ever pulled off around here and it is to be hoped that Mr. Brush will get proper protection for the Cubs when they come here again.

Baseball is baseball, and if the Giants couldn't win fairly there should be no win otherwise.

No one who saw the game could say that the umpires were sore at McGraw. Some decisions seemed to favor the local players and if with that and the rowdyism they couldn't win, the game should go to the better team. New York had everything in its favor.

They were playing on the home ground, they had the crowd and umpires with them, the other team had spent the night on the cars coming here. Matty, the greatest pitcher we ever had, was in the box and the whole team was right, except for a few scratched skins. What more could a fellow ask for?

McGinnity started a row the very first thing by bumping Chance off the plate while the latter was hitting out flies. That was only the first incident. Once when Kling was chasing a foul from Doyle's bat, two beer bottles, a drinking glass and a derby hat were thrown at him.

Is that baseball? Does that do New York any good?

Gee whiz! If we can't lose a pennant without dirty work let's quit altogether.

— Tad, New York *Evening Journal*

The Cubs will be acknowledged as champions, but their title is tainted, and New York lovers of baseball will never acknowledge them as the true winners of the pennant.

Whenever I mention the Giants from now on I shall accord them their rightful title, and I am firm in the opinion that I am right.

Yesterday they looked outclassed for the reason that they were far from being in the playing form the Cubs were. It cannot be denied that the Chicago players were far fresher and in better shape for such a crucial contest after their several days' rest than were the Giants, who were forced to play their very best up to the very day before the deciding game.

If those men on the Board of Directors had concocted a scheme to give the Giants the worst of it they couldn't have done it any more to the point. The Giants were not outgamed, but they were outplayed just from lack of condition.

The Giants did not play up-to-date baseball either. They should almost have cinched the victory in the first inning, for with men on first and second and none out, Bresnahan, instead of trying to advance the runners, tried to knock the cover off the ball and fanned. Herzog then made a play that possibly lost all chances the Giants had. When Kling dropped Bresnahan's third strike, possibly purposely, for Johnny Kling is a very foxy player, Herzog made a break for second although Bresnahan was already out whether Kling held the ball or not. Kling took advantage of Herzog's dumbness and threw to Chance and "Herzie" was pinched. As Donlin followed with a double, it can be seen how damaging Herzog's mistake was.

The minute that "Miner" Brown took Pfiester's place in the box, that strange fatality that has always followed Matty when against the great three-fingered boxman bobbed up and "Big Six" got his bumps.

— Sam Crane, New York *Evening Journal*

BUFFALO, OCT. 9 — The world's champion Cubs are rushing to Detroit to meet the Tigers tomorrow and defend their title.

Frank Chance's Cubs have proven their title as the greatest aggregation ever gathered on a diamond, game, true and loyal to the core.

Chance was not seriously hurt when hit in the throat by a spectator on his way to the clubhouse. It broke a cartilage in his throat and pained him a good deal, but physicians assured him there was nothing serious about the injury, and he ate a hearty dinner last night. Steinfeldt was struck in the face at the same time Chance was hit, and Hofman was hit in the nose by a pop bottle hurled by an irate fan.

Telegrams of congratulations poured in on the club as it was rushing out of New York last night, including a message from Judge Kenesaw M. Landis. The one most appreciated was this message from Barney Dreyfuss: "Hearty congratulations. Clean baseball was bound to triumph over affidavits and rowdyism. Best wishes for success in world's series."

— Chicago *News*

Great are the Cubs and nearly as great are their fans.

Yesterday they massed themselves in Orchestra Hall, where the *Tribune* baseball board pictured the plays, a howling, shrieking, ball-mad crowd, wild in its enthusiasm, sometimes pleading, sometimes threatening, always "pulling."

Through it all sat a handsome young woman whose eyes shone and cheeks flushed as the cheering increased, and who, when the Giants retired at the close of the ninth, turned to the gray-haired woman by her side and said:

"This is our anniversary day, mother. He had to win. It's

wonderful, isn't it?" and she laughed and cried at the same time.

If the crowd had known that the wife of the great Cub leader was in their midst, Mrs. Frank Le Roy Chance would have been given an ovation that seldom falls to the lot of a woman.

Another Cub wife was in the throng. With a party of friends Mrs. "Joe" Tinker sat only a few rows behind Mrs. Chance, madly waving a Cub banner.

Upon leaving the building she shouted over and over:
"Four to two, four to two."

— Chicago *Tribune*

"We will beat Detroit easily," declared Mrs. Frank Chance last night, previous to boarding a train for the scene of tomorrow's battle. The wife of the Cubs' captain was excited and in a hurry to depart.

"I want to help Frank beard the Tigers in their lair," she said smiling. "I know we will win, but Frank says he always plays better ball when he can see me in the grandstand. Of course that is silly, but I want to be there just the same."

"You certainly have a chance," a friend suggested.

"Now, I think that's real mean of you," pouted the young woman. "You know everyone tells me that, but as a pun I think it is awful.

"Just as soon as the season is over and we have demonstrated to Detroit that they are not in our class, Mr. Chance and I plan a fishing trip to Wisconsin. He is very fond of fishing, and so am I. Then we are going to California for the winter.

"Yes, we like Chicago, but those lake winds are fearfully chilly in the winter. California is the place for winter months. Besides, Mr. Chance has so many friends there. He formerly attended Washington College in that state and was offered a scholarship at Leland Stanford to play football. He played football but did not like it as much as baseball."

Mrs. Chance, young, pretty and with a large quantity of light brown hair, was recognized by a number of persons and several women stepped forward, introduced themselves and wished that her husband might have all sorts of luck in the championship games.

— Chicago *Journal*

Manager McGraw took things philosophically.

"I do not feel badly," McGraw said. "My team merely lost something it had honestly won three weeks ago. This cannot be put too strongly: Chicagoans always will remember the fight I gave them before they could gain their third pennant in succession."

— New York *Press*

Probably no member of the Giants took the defeat as keenly as did Christy Mathewson. Long after the other players had donned their street clothes and made for home Matty sat down disconsolate in the dressing room.

Folks that lingered tried to cheer the peerless pitcher, but he could not speak. He seemed loath to go out and face the people. Some few of the faithful remained until toward dusk, when the great pitcher showed at the Eighth avenue gate. He got a cheer that must have gone a great way in uplifting his fallen spirits.

Matty tried to speak but couldn't. He waved at the crowd and hurried away with bowed head. "I did the best I could," he said as he left the clubhouse, "but I guess fate was against me."

— New York *American*

Bridwell was the only member of the New York team to offer the Cubs congratulations after their victory yesterday.

— Chicago *Journal*

A people who can become as excited about anything as the majority of New Yorkers can about the baseball pennant is far from being lost to hope.

Were we a wooden, lethargic populace, incapable of caring a rap whether the pennant of 1908 fluttered over the Polo

Grounds or held horizontal in the breeze that sweeps over Lake Michigan, we might well account ourselves unworthy of the terrific work that must be done before the Augean stable of municipal rottenness has been cleaned.

But we know now that we can become excited, energetically, masterfully excited, and as soon as we understand how properly to apply that tremendous dynamite force to the really important things of life, we will get what we ought to have, individually and collectively, and no thieving corporations, no swinish bosses, no bludgeon-bearing election thieves can stand a minute before us.

Today a multitude of men are bewailing the grewsome [*sic*] fact that Merkle did not run to second in that tie game. That omission cost New York the pennant. It was a common error, the slovenly heedlessness that keeps most of mankind in its rut, and exalts the men who play the game, be it business, or love, or war, to the bitter end.

Merkle's blunder cost New York the pennant. True. This does not lower the price of beef; it does not make travel on the Third avenue "L" any less hazardous; it does not save the old from toil or the poor from hunger. It affects not one jot the status of any of the hundreds of thousands who were wrought up over the victory that has been borne away to Chicago.

But it evoked excitement. No human being in New York yesterday can deny that. And excitement makes the world go round; causes the pulse to beat higher, the thrill of battle to rouse the sluggish blood, the brain to do ten times the work it can do when plodding along in emotionless tranquility.

And in that possibility of enthusiasm lies the certainty of the future.

The day will come when the people of this city will be just as excited about the struggle over the rights of the masses, just as enthusiastic over the fight between public plunderers and their protesting prey; in brief, just as interested in the things that concern them, and concern them vitally, as in the settlement of a baseball championship, involving personally a handful of men.

When that day comes there will be trouble for public despoilers, long repentant years in jail for criminal bosses, and an epidemic of public welfare such as now seems too Utopian even to dream of.

This newspaper, being loyal to New York, chronicles its sorrow that the pennant has been rudely taken from us. But it rejoices in the patent fact that the people of New York are capable of tumultuous enthusiasm, for in that it sees the hope of every betterment that it has earnestly and honestly sought to bring about.

— Editorial page, New York *American*

Final National League Standings

	W	L	PCT.	GB
Chicago	99	55	.643	—
New York	98	56	.636	1
Pittsburgh	98	56	.636	1
Philadelphia	83	71	.539	16
Cincinnati	73	81	.474	26
Boston	63	91	.409	36
Brooklyn	53	101	.344	46
St. Louis	49	105	.318	50

Postscript

In the world series of 1908, Chicago beat Detroit, four games to one. Chicago's winning pitchers: Brown (games one and four), and Overall (games two and five). The only home run in the series was hit by Joe Tinker in game two.

On July 19, 1909, in New York City, National League President Harry Pulliam committed suicide. Since the end of the 1908 season he had taken a leave of absence from his job, because of a severe state of depression, which, his doctors said, had been brought on by the turmoil that followed the Giant–Cub game of September 23.

Gabby Hartnett as told to Hal Totten

1938: Chicago Cubs 6, Pittsburgh Pirates 5

Chicago Sun-Times

Do you know how you feel when you're real scared, or something BIG is going to happen? Well, that's the way I felt for one terrific minute of my biggest day in baseball — and I don't believe you'll have to guess very much as to just which day that was.

It was in 1938, Sept. 28, the day of "the home run in the dark." But as a matter of fact, that day — that one big moment — was the climax of a series of things that had gone on for a week or more. And every one of those incidents helped to make it the biggest day in all my years in the major leagues.

The week before — on Sunday — you'll remember we had played a double-header in Brooklyn. We lost the first game 4 to 3, and we were leading the second game by two runs along about the fifth inning. It was muddy and raining and was getting dark fast. Then big Fred Sington came up with a man on base and hit a home run to tie the score.

It was too dark to play any more, so they called the game and it ended in a tie. Now — every game meant a lot to us just then. We were three and a half games behind. Winning was the only way we could hope to catch the Pirates. And we were scheduled in Philadelphia the next day. So we couldn't play the game off then.

But MacPhail wanted to play it. We had an open date for travel at the end of the series in Philly, and he wanted us to go back to Brooklyn and play off the tie. The boys wanted to play it, too. They figured we could win it and gain on the Pirates.

Well, I couldn't make up my mind right away, so I asked MacPhail to give me 24 hours to decide. He said he would. But I'd been figuring — you see, we had to win all three games in the series with Pittsburgh if we were to win the pennant. And I had to think of my pitchers. I had to argue with the whole ball club — they wanted to play.

But I stuck my neck out and turned it down. I'll admit that I didn't feel any too easy about it. But I had to make the decision. And I felt that we might lose that game just as easy as we could win it. So I took that chance.

Well, we sat for three days in Philly and watched it rain. Of course, Pittsburgh wasn't able to play in Brooklyn, either. And they were three and a half games in front of us. On Thursday we played the Phils twice and beat 'em both times, 4 to 0 and 2 to 1. Lee won his 20th game of the season in that first one — and his fourth straight shutout. Clay Bryant was the pitcher in the second. But Pittsburgh beat Brooklyn twice, so we were still three and a half back.

The next day we won two again — and we had to come from behind to do it. Rip Collins put the second one on ice by doubling in the ninth with the bases full to drive in three runs just as they posted the score showing that Cincinnati had beaten the Pirates. That put us within two games of the leaders. We were really rollin'.

Then we came home and on Saturday we played the Cardinals — and beat 'em 9 to 3. But the Pirates won, too. On Sunday it was the same thing — we both won. Monday Pittsburgh wasn't scheduled, so the Pirates were in the stands at Wrigley Field as we played the final of the series with St. Louis. Bill Lee was scored on for the first time in five games, but we won 6 to 3. And then came the big series — with the lead cut to a game and a half.

I stuck my neck out in the very first game of the series. Several times, in fact. I started Dizzy Dean on the mound. He hadn't pitched since Sept. 13 and hadn't started a game since Aug. 13. But how he pitched! Just a slow ball, control, and a world of heart.

We got him out in front in the third when Collins tripled and Jurges drove him in with a single. For five innings Dean was superb. Then he seemed to tire. Not due to anything that happened on the field.

Lloyd Waner grounded out in that inning, and Paul Waner fouled out. Rizzo singled, but Vaughan popped to Herman. Still, I noticed that he didn't have as much on the ball.

Probably I was the only one to notice it — except maybe Diz himself. I began to worry a bit. And I made up my mind right then and there that no matter how anything else was going, the minute Dean got in trouble, I was going to get him out of there. We got another run the last half of that inning. And Diz got through the seventh and eighth, although it took a great play by Dean himself to cut down a run at the plate in the eighth.

When the ninth came around I decided to play safe and started Lee warming up in the bull pen. Bill wasn't usually a good relief pitcher, but he was the best pitcher in the league, and that was a spot for the best we had.

Dean hit Vaughan to start the ninth and I was plenty uneasy. But Suhr popped out, and Jensen batted for Young and forced Arky at second. Then came little "Jeep" Handley and he hit one clear to the wall in left center for a double. That put the tying runs on second and third, and that was my cue.

Todd was up. He always hit Dean pretty good, even when Diz had his stuff — and Diz didn't have a thing then. Not only that, but Todd never hit Lee very well. So even though Lee hadn't been a steady relief pitcher, I called him in. My neck was out again. What if Todd hit one? What if Lee had trouble getting started — after all, he'd been working day after day. But — well, when it gets to the place where it means a ball game, you've got to make a change, even if the hitter socks one into the bleachers.

I'll say this for Dean — he never complained about that. He walked right in and said I'd done the right thing — that he'd lost his stuff and his arm didn't feel so good. So Lee came in. The first pitch was a strike. Todd fouled the next one off. Then Lee cut loose with as wild a pitch as I ever saw and Jensen scored. Handley went to third with the tying run. My hunch didn't look so good. But Lee wound up again; he pitched; and Todd swung and struck out. We'd won the game and were only a half game out of first place.

That brings us up to the big day. We scored in the second inning on a couple of errors. But Pittsburgh went ahead with three in the sixth. We tied it up in our half. But the Pirates got two in the eighth and led, 5 to 3. In our half Collins opened with a single and Jurges walked.

Lazzeri batted for Lee, who had gone in again that day, and doubled, scoring Rip. They walked Hack. Then Herman drove in Jurges to tie it up again, but Joe Marty — who had run for Tony — was thrown out at the plate by Paul Waner. A double play ended that round.

It was very dark by then. But the umpires decided to let us go one more. Charlie Root got through the first half of the ninth all right. In our half Cavarretta hit one a country mile to center, but Lloyd Waner pulled it down. Reynolds grounded out. And it was my turn.

Well — I swung once — and missed; I swung again, and got a piece of it, but that was all. A foul and strike two. I had one more chance. Mace Brown wound up and let fly; I swung with everything I had and then I got that feeling I was talking about — the kind of feeling you get when the blood rushes out of your head and you get dizzy.

A lot of people have told me they didn't know the ball was in the bleachers. Well I did — maybe I was the only one in the park who did. I knew it the minute I hit it. When I got to second base I couldn't see third for the players and fans there. I don't think I walked a step to the plate — I was carried in. But when I got there I saw George Barr taking a good look — he was going to make sure I touched that platter.

That was the shot that did it. We went into first place. And while we still had the pennant to win, we couldn't be headed. We won again the next day for Bill Lee, easy — 10 to 1. The heart was gone out of Pittsburgh. And we clinched the pennant down in St. Louis the next Saturday when we won and Pittsburgh lost to Cincinnati.

David Condon

The Summer of '45

Chicago Tribune, May 21–23, 1972

For every country boy suddenly loosed in a major league city, there has been a summer of '45.

That summer of '45. What Chicago Cub fan who thrilled thru it can ever forget?

World War II ended that August. Only vaguely, tho, do I recall our kissing and drinking along Michigan Boulevard, from the Old Continental Hotel to the old Stevens, on V-J night. At the Morrison Hotel in the Loop, a pretty girl seized the ruptured-duck discharge pin from my lapel.

The baseball summer of '45 was something else. I was 21, and it was a part of me.

It was the Cubs' World Series season, and I was a part of it.

So was my pal, Vince Garrity, former Cub batboy and almost unknown soldier. Garrity conned a Series ticket in the box of United States Senator A. B. [Happy] Chandler.

But this was all right with Chandler. The baseball summer of '45 belonged to Happy, too. It was Happy's first World Series after succeeding baseball's original and only czar, Judge Kenesaw M. Landis.

The summer of '45 was Cy Block's and Eddie Hanyzewski's. The later era Bleacher Bums would have canonized this picturesque pair.

Hanyzewski, from the South Bend sandlots, received a full $3,930.22 losers' share tho he didn't pitch in the Series.

Block flunked his only World Series pinch-hit assignment against Detroit's Tigers. His $250 swag was $50 short of what Cy spent to return to a Cub uniform when he discarded military rompers.

Cy did better in the money league after his 17-game Cub career ended. He almost bought the Tigers with a $5 million bid in 1956. So 11 years from now will Joe Pepitone bid for the Cubs?

Oh, that summer of '45. It belonged to those of us at Union Station, on Oct. 5, welcoming or on the night train bearing our heroes from Detroit. With the Cubs came a 2-games-to-1 series lead.

But the Union Station crowd was no more rabid than Hi Bithorn's homefolks down in Puerto Rico. They inundated Manager Charlie Grimm with telegrams to pitch the blubbery Bithorn, another eligible service returnee. Herr Charlie apparently couldn't read Spanish.

It was '45, and Bert Wilson's greatest summer. Tho the likeable microphone maniac is long dead, his chant re-echoes: "I don't care who wins as long as it's the Cubs!"

Somehow, at 48, you don't get the same effect from Jack Brickhouse's "Hey! Hey!"

Chicago, baseball, the announcers, and the players have changed faces since that summer when beautiful Wrigley Field was beautiful.

The Continental Hotel is the Sheraton-Chicago. The Stevens is the Conrad Hilton. The Morrison survives only in memories of Soldier Farr and the Cook County Democratic Committee.

Wrigley Field remains the sole 1945 National League arena still luring fans. Elsewhere, baseball has changed so much.

The Braves fled from Boston to Milwaukee to Atlanta. Ebbets Field is a housing project. Its colorful old Bums are gentlemen tenants of posh Chavez Ravine in Los Angeles. The Giants are in San Francisco, and it took Willie Mays' return to New York — courtesy of the upstart Mets — to jog recollections of the Polo Grounds and an age that used to be.

There is a new club in San Diego, or there was yesterday.

Houston's Astrodome is too rich for my blood. I still regard Montreal as a hockey town, and the baseball Expos have done little to disturb that notion.

Vince Lloyd and Lou Boudreau share Wilson's former radio booth. This tandem now earns practically the $100,000 sum that Mutual Network paid for exclusive broadcast rights to the '45 Series.

We had no TV then. But last Thursday night I watched the Cub telecast from Atlanta. They showed me an infield of Hickman, Beckert, Kessinger, Fanzone.

Somehow, the picture seemed fuzzy. I kept seeing the faces of Phil Cavarretta, Don Johnson, Roy Hughes, Stan Hack, and their magnificent mates of the summer of '45.

I see those faces once again. In reverie I see them as plainly as from the general admission seats that cost 25 cents each with tax passes.

Those passes were courtesy of Irving Vaughan and Edward Burns, magnificent writers who both left fortunes, and, I suppose, shoeboxes full of unused tax tickets.

The newspaper business, as well as baseball, was different then. A baseball writer had the most prestigious job in *The Tribune* sports department. He suspected each newcomer of starting a death watch on him. He certainly was not about to encourage the development of another baseball addict in his own department. When it came to tickets, he gave like a steel beam.

Unless they were for his butcher, who'd get box seat comps.

But Vaughan and Burns became my friends. More than that, in the summer of '45 they were my non-playing heroes. With a genuine affection for the game, they were biographers of players whose faces I now see:

Philibuck Cavarretta, Stan Hack, Claude Passeau, Hank Wyse, Paul Derringer, Heinz Becker, Andy Pafko, Peanuts Lowrey, Swish Nicholson.

But two faces are more vivid than the others. I see them as clearly as I hear the growling of Traveling Secretary Bob Lewis, sentinel of the pass gate.

They are the faces of Hank Borowy and Jim Gallagher, the two who made possible the summer of '45.

General manager Gallagher executed the coup bringing Henry Ludwig Borowy, a right-handed Yankee pitcher, to the Cubs late in July. The Cubs, in first place since July 8, sought a way to preserve that lead. Gallagher found it.

Searching the Yankee waiver list, Gallagher saw that Walt Dubiel and Ernie Bonham would be available. Their price tags were approximately $50,000 each. Gallagher asked Scout Jack Doyle to appraise Dubiel and Bonham.

"Neither's worth a quarter," reported Doyle. Gallagher telephoned the Yankees' fiery chieftain, Larry MacPhail, that there was no deal.

"Soon we had an off-day. I went fishing with Grimm, Passeau, and Hard Rock [Roy] Johnson," Gallagher remembers. "I got back late, and full of beer. I had to return an urgent call from MacPhail.

"MacPhail offered Borowy for $75,000 and two players worth $12,500 each. Actually, he was asking $100,000 for a pitcher who in spring had started developing a knuckler because his curve had faded to a wrinkle.

"MacPhail wanted an immediate answer and assured me the Yankees had waivers on Borowy. I was hesitant about spending Mr. Wrigley's money. Grimm didn't know anything about the American League, so I went to Doyle again. He said it was worth the risk."

Borowy won 11 games and lost only two as the Cubs blazed home. Meanwhile, MacPhail kept demanding two players.

"Where could anyone find two extra players those days?" says Gallagher. "We finally sent the Yankees another check; for $25,000. MacPhail wasn't very happy."

Borowy pitched the Cubs to a 9–0 victory in the World Series opener. The next Cub starters were Wyse, Passeau, and Pappy Prim. Borowy didn't pitch again until game No. 5. And No. 6, and No. 7. He was Chicago's pitcher of record in all three concluding contests!

Today, Hanyzewski, pensioned from the South Bend police

department, is a high school security officer. Block is a wealthy New York investment official. The murdered Bithorn rests in a grave in Puerto Rico. Borowy has a real estate business in Bloomfield, N.J., and often strolls around his cottage on the Jersey Shores.

When Hank strolls, does he sometimes recall this picture: First inning of the final World Series game the summer of '45. Skeeter Webb and Eddie Mayo of the Tigers on base. None out. Doc Cramer batting. Borowy pitching . . . weary, weary, weary.

The summer of '45, when I came of age to buy beer, was a heady one in Wrigley Field. Baseball was the intoxicant.

Even going to the Cubs' park was adventuresome because I rode the Clark Street surface cars, an experience likened to Russian Roulette with a carbine.

Street cars and sports writers of '45 were of varied vintage and unpredictable performance. So were the Cubs.

For example: Lennie Merullo, Paul Derringer, and, tho it be heresy, my immortal Bill [Swish] Nicholson.

Merullo was no Joe Tinker at shortstop. Not even in the championship year of 1945, when Tinker was 65. Lennie had a son nicknamed Boots, born Sept. 13, 1942. That was the day Merullo pere accomplished four errors in a single inning.

Derringer was a picturesque favorite. The stories about Oom Paul were as fascinating as his record.

There was the tale of his battle with Cincinnati's Larry MacPhail, who later moved to the Yankees. When Derringer allegedly fireballed an inkstand at MacPhail's head, the white-faced MacPhail gasped: "You could have killed me."

Derringer, never a Dale Carnegie, replied: "That's just what I was aimin' to do." If that story about Derringer isn't completely true, it's one of the few.

Twenty-seven years ago it never occurred to me that men aged, an oversight subsequently corrected. All summer I anticipated that Derringer finally would dazzle us with the pitching magic that had qualified him for previous World Series ventures.

A Cardinal in 1931, Derringer lost two decisions to the powerhouse Athletics and Lefty Grove.

Against the bombshell Yankees of '39, Oom Paul started twice for Cincinnati, where he had landed in a trade dispatching Leo Durocher to the Cardinals.

Oom Paul twice twisted the Tigers' tails, and Bobo Newsom's and Dizzy Trout's, too, for Cincinnati in '40. (He broke even in a pair with Bobo.)

Came marvelous 1945. The night before the seventh game, newsmen sat in Eddie Siegel's saloon — an oasis since devoured by Riccardo's — and pondered the Cubs' mauled mound staff. I declared Derringer would be a surprise starter in the morrow's point-of-no-return contest.

The forecast narrowly missed. Hank Borowy lame-armed only nine pitches before Manager Charlie Grimm summoned Derringer, 39 summers old. Paul cluttered the runways with even more Tigers.

Nicholson was Wrigley Field's Ernie Banks of that period, altho he slumped to 13 home runs in '45. He also failed me in game No. 7.

At Siegel's saloon, I forecast that a Nicholson home run heroic would win the decisive game and the Cubs' first world championship since 1908.

Swish let us down. The Cubs, in fact, never collected another home run after Phil Cavarretta's in the opener.

Cavarretta batted .423, and Stan Hack hit .367, against a Tiger pitching corps that starred Prince Hal Newhouser, Dizzy Trout, Virgil Trucks, and Stubby Overmire.

The varsity catcher for Detroit was Paul Rapier Richards. No one dreamed Richards would return to Chicago six years afterwards to revitalize the White Sox.

Richards managed the White Sox less than four seasons. Still, that was sufficient span for Richards to watch the Cubs' field generalship pass from Frank Frisch to Cavarretta to Hack.

In '45, we frequently speculated whether Philibuck or Stanislaus would receive first crack at managing our Cub club. When their turns ultimately came, neither showed us anything like that summer of '45.

That summer of '45, a few other young lodgers at Lawson Y.M.C.A. did not share my enthusiasm for Wrigley Field. They preferred afternoons at Oak Street Beach.

The beach scenery was better. Many times, so was the action. This assured that our town's population maintained a certain stability despite the Clark Street motormen's zeal for decimating it.

But tho the beachfront offered counter-attractions, Wrigley Field was my Mecca and the Cubs were my gods. All of 'em, including Mickey Livingston, Paul Gillespie, and Harry (Peanuts) Lowrey, a trio who wore the returned serviceman's ruptured duck insignia on their uniforms' left sleeves.

Wrigley Field had been my Mecca since childhood in New Mexico when Grandpa Condon — who had asylumed on Goose Island during the Chicago fire — needed assistance to read the Cub box scores in his mail edition of the *Chicago Tribune*.

Grandpa's eyesight began failing in 1932. That year I read him Cub World Series boxes that included the names of Charlie Grimm, Lon Warneke, and Stan Hack.

We continued *The Tribune* after Grandpa died. When Grimm managed the Cubs into the '35 series, the names of Warneke and Hack again loomed in the box scores. Cavarretta's had been added.

Grimm and Warneke were elsewhere during the Cubs' World Series of 1938. Then, suddenly, it was summer of '45, and this buckwheat was spending his afternoons at Wrigley Field.

Jolly Cholly Grimm was back as manager. Cavarretta and Hack still cornered the infield. Warneke quit his retirement home in Arkansas near mid-season. From July 8, we sensed a World Series.

What a summer! What a Series, even with wartime personnel. On Oct. 10, the series came to the seventh game all square. A standing room crowd of 41,590 was in bunting-bedecked Wrigley Field. The National Anthem echoed.

Then weary Hank Borowy, making his fourth appearance of the festival, faced Skeeter Webb, former White Sox infielder and Detroit's leadoff hitter. Webb singled on a 3–2 pitch. Eddie Mayo singled on Borowy's first offering. Webb scored on Dock Cramer's single over third.

Here comes my man, Oom Paul Derringer, to relieve Borowy!

Hank Greenberg, whose grand-slam homer on the season's final day qualified Detroit for this series, caused no trouble for Derringer. Roy Cullenbine was purposely passed. Bases filled.

The double play did not develop but Derringer was happier after dangerous Rudy York popped up. Jimmy Outlaw, a .167 hitter at this point in the Series, approached the plate.

We practically were out of the inning at the cost of only one run. However:

Derringer walked Outlaw, forcing in Mayo. Detroit 2, Chicago 0. Richards' double evacuated the bases and it was 5–0. Suddenly, Cub fans felt the raw chill of fall. Summer of '45 was over.

A few days later, while Detroit still celebrated its 9–3 championship victory, Derringer encountered Jim Gallagher, the Cubs' general manager. Gallagher says Derringer told him: "It's funny, Jim. That's the first time I ever walked in a run!"

"That blankety-blank thought it was funny!" Gallagher roared recently. "After 27 years, I still don't."

It wasn't funny. In retrospect, tho, even losing the Series was fun. The Cubs won three games, matching their victory total in four previous Series appearances since losing to Boston and Babe Ruth in 1918. Two of those '45 triumphs were historical.

The World Series climaxing the summer of '45 was a most unusual one. For openers, consider that four-sevenths of it was committed in beautiful Wrigley Field.

Which disproves any notion that the North Side is zoned against baseball's post-season tournament. It has only seemed that way.

But did Handy Andy Pafko, Hy Vandenberg, Ed Sauer, Paul Erickson, Heinz Becker, Bob Chipman, Dewey Williams, and the rest of Jolly Cholly's Cub crew win the darned thing? Next question, please. The '45 Series wasn't that unusual.

For me, tho, it was sufficient that the Cubs pushed the Series into maximum overtime.

Thanks to nifty hurling by Hank Borowy and Claude Passeau, and some weird english on Stan Hack's bounding double in game No. 6, the Cubs achieved three thrilling triumphs.

As James Thurber suggested in his equally improbable story of the baseball midget, you could look it up.

Look it up. The 1945 Series was more unusual than 1918, when Babe Ruth pitched Boston to victory in a baseball bakeoff that saw the Cubs borrowing Comiskey Park.

So what if there was a short-lived strike in that 1918 Series? The Cubs threatened a strike in '45.

The Cubs' unusual Series of 1932 also featured Babe Ruth, by then a Yankee and Sultan of Swat.

Ruth made that Series historical by signalling — to pitcher Charley Root and 49,986 Wrigley Field fans — exactly when and where he would deliver a home run. Tho a Cub player gratefully said "we're lucky we weren't killed" it wasn't as unusual a Series as the '45 festival.

Nor was even the Series of 1929, marked by Hack Wilson losing Mule Haas' fly ball in the sun for a bargain-basement homer while the Athletics were engineering a 10-run inning against the Cubs.

Wilson's blunder earned him a niche with Heinie Zimmerman, Johnny Miljus, Mickey Owen, and similar Series goats.

But the most famous goat in Series history didn't show until '45. This was a live, genuinely fragrant goat named Sonovia. It's likely because of Sonovia that Wrigley Field hasn't seen a Series since.

Even the World Series game pattern detoured tradition in '45. Because wartime travel restrictions still were in effect, three consecutive games were scheduled for Detroit, the opening site.

This technically was to the Tigers' advantage, and was so noted by James Carroll, the St. Louis betting commissioner. Carroll made Detroit backers wager $13 to risk winning $10. Sportswriters favored the Tigers, 45 votes to 35, with Warren Brown abstaining.

"I don't think either team can win it," said Brown. "I've seen 'em both play."

If the Tigers did have an edge in their home lair, the secret did not leak to our Cubs.

The Cubs chased Pitcher Hal Newhouser for a 9–0 opening game victory behind Hank Borowy, finessed from the American League only weeks earlier. Detroit got to Hank Wyse, a 22-game winner, for a 4–1 conquest in the second contest.

The Series was deadlocked. Warren Brown's opinion seemed credible until the Cubs tossed a third consecutive right-hander at Detroit.

He was Claude William Passeau. Claude, 34, consistently had posted twin-figure victory totals in the six seasons since the Cubs grabbed him from the Phillies for Joe Marty, Kirby Higbe, and Ray Harrell. Now Passeau neared his finest hour.

Just 28 Tigers faced Passeau. Rudy York's second inning single was Detroit's only hit. Bob Swift drew Passeau's sole walk and was a double play victim.

It was the most spectacular World Series pitching performance in history, up to that point. Cub Ed Reulbach's one-hitter against the '06 White Sox was suspect because of lax scoring rules. Besides, Ed walked six Sox.

The Yankees' Bill Bevens almost surpassed Passeau's feat two years later. Bevens had a no-hitter until Brooklyn's Cookie Lavagetto bagged a pinch double with two out in the ninth. Since Bevens lost that 1947 one-hitter, Passeau's glory was not overshadowed until Yankee Don Larsen posted a perfect game in 1956.

I saw Larsen's masterpiece. Its main effect was to bring back memories of Passeau.

Memories of the summer of '45 are magnificent.

Enter the goat! Jolly Cholly Grimm's Cubs were happy to escape Detroit. They had been quartered in four different hotels. And a strike had been prospect until Bob Lewis, the traveling secretary, moved the wives from lake steamer accommodations to those inns.

Happy fans greeted the happy warriors' train at Union Station. One of the merriest fans was William [Billy Goat] Sianis, keeper of the saloon and of a prominent herd of goats. Billy had unique intentions.

Gov. Dwight Green was in Wrigley Field the next afternoon. Mayor Ed Kelly was present, too. Mr. Billy Goat Sianis and his blue-ribbon goat, Sonovia, also appeared.

Mr. Sianis presented a pair of box seat tickets and escorted Sonovia to choice pews. The Frain ushers started squawking on those new fangled handy-talkies and very quickly both goats, Billy and Sonovia, were being rushed exitwise. Sonovia's ticket was retrieved. Presently it is mounted in the Billy Goat Inn, more prominent than pictures of the many Pulitzer Prize winners who patronize Billy Goat's Chicago Club North.

When the Tigers surged ahead by winning the fourth and fifth games, Billy Goat placed an eternal hex on the Cubs. As an afterthought, he telegraphed Owner Philip K. Wrigley: "Who smells now?"

Wrigley passed the games in Detroit to answer ticket complaints personally. Jaunting to his own park, Wrigley was stopped at the stiles by One-Eyed Connolly, a temporary usher. Very temporary, it turned out.

The sixth game soothed Wrigley's feelings tho he fretted until the Cubs' 12th. Then, with two out and Bill Schuster running for Pinch Hitter Frank Secory, Stan Hack belted Dizzy Trout's 1–2 pitch.

Shades of 1924, when a most costly 12th inning Series bingle bounced over New York's Fred Lindstrom! Hack's drive skipped over Hank Greenberg, whose earlier home run had created a 7–7 deadlock. Schuster scored from first. The Series was even.

A day of rest that followed wasn't sufficient for fatigued Hank Borowy. Making his fourth appearance, Borowy was the Cub loser in No. 7.

So concluded the magnificent summer of '45.

A quarter-century, plus, has elapsed. The Series since has visited sites not even in the majors in 1945: Milwaukee, Baltimore, Los Angeles, San Francisco, Minnesota, the miracle Mets' Shea Stadium. But it hasn't returned to Wrigley Field.

Billy Goat's hex reaches out from the grave.

Skip Myslenski

All the Laughter Died
in Sorrow

Chicago Tribune, June 8, 1979

That year unfolded capriciously, each of us caught on an un-
dulating ride, the unimaginable loosed on our worlds. A new
president continued an old war, and a nation rocked with con-
vulsions. A new world was opened when Neil Armstrong
walked across the moon.

Mighty people died: a past president, Dwight D. Eisen-
hower; a senator, Everett Dirksen; an enemy, Ho Chi Minh;
and a hero, Rocky Marciano. Bernadette Devlin, a fiery
sprite of a girl, emerged as a new spokesperson for Northern
Ireland, but Charles de Gaulle, his regal mien shaken by
defeat, abdicated in France. The last of another royal family,
the Kennedys, also made news, at a small bridge on Chappa-
quiddick Island.

"Memory," the novelist Graham Greene once wrote, "is
like a long broken night." But with these recollections of controversy, confusion, death, awe, and outrage stands another.
It, too, would end in despair, but through a spring and a
summer it offered hope for even the wildest of dreams. For
in that year of 1969, the Chicago Cubs chased a championship.

That season marked the beginning of baseball's second
century, and for the first time the majors were expanded to
24 teams and each league was split into two divisions. Mickey

Mantle had finally ended an 18-year career. Hoyt Wilhelm, age 45, was still around, though, and so was 37-year-old Ernie Banks, who prepared for this season as he always did, by spending two weeks at the Buckhorn Spa near Mesa, Ariz.

Leo Durocher, the manager, passed much of his winter in Acapulco. "The Cubs are now ready to go for all the marbles . . ." he wrote in a letter that was published in the *Chicago American.* "It figures to be a mighty interesting season, and I wouldn't be surprised if the Cubs are the ones who make it just that."

Ron Santo, the third baseman, reported to spring training at 198 pounds, his lightest weight. Catcher Randy Hundley was lighter, too, after an off-season of lifting weights and eating a high-protein diet. "The last couple of years I spent more time working on my catching and my hitting fell off," he declared. "But this spring I've spent a lot of extra time in the batting cage and . . . I'm not lunging at the ball as much as I used to and I feel my bat is quicker."

The pitchers, however, were developing more slowly, their progress hindered by a threatened players' strike (which kept them out of camp for 10 days) and by the unusually cold and wet weather in Scottsdale, Ariz.

Alec Distaso, one of those pitchers, was being compared to Don Drysdale, but he eventually floundered and was sent to the minors. Adolfo Phillips, a center fielder, had already been characterized as the new Willie Mays, but he fractured his right hand in March and was replaced by Oscar Gamble, who was 18 years old and had only 34 games of professional experience. "Gamble's my center fielder," Durocher announced on the day of Phillips' injury, and when he was questioned about this, he merely snorted, "What's a matter? Did ya ever hear of Ott and Frisch? They didn't need any experience. They started right off in the big leagues."

Oscar Gamble wouldn't, and within two weeks he was sent down. The job suddenly belonged to an anonymous 22-year-old named Don Young.

The Cubs debut in Wrigley Field before their largest

opening day crowd since 1929, and they defeat the Philadelphia Phillies, 7–6. Ernie Banks crushes two home runs and
has five runs batted in, but the victory is not secured until the
11th, when Willie Smith — a former boxer and a former
pitcher — pinch hits for Jim Hickman and delivers a two-run
homer.

They will rattle off four straight victories, then lose to the
Expos, then win seven more, their successes precipitated by
a bevy of stars. In their second game Billy Williams strokes
four doubles, tying a major league record; in their third game
the slimmer Santo hits two homers; in their fourth game Joe
Niekro and Ted Abernathy combine to pitch a 12-inning
shutout. They win their fifth with three runs in the ninth,
their sixth behind a shutout by Holtzman, their seventh
behind 4⅔ innings of shutout relief by Hank Aguirre and
Abernathy, their eighth behind a five-hit shutout by Ferguson
Jenkins, their ninth behind a shutout by Bill Hands and Phil
Regan, and their 10th behind five innings of shutout relief by
Regan and Abernathy.

On April 14, after their seventh game of the season, they
find themselves alone in first place. They will stay there for
149 days.

The madness in the far reaches of Wrigley Field also has
started early, and the legendary exploits of The Bleacher
Bums are already being spread. They are a marauding troupe,
a raucous group that was spawned three years ago, and now
they have a president, identifiable garb (yellow hardhats), a
head cheerleader (pitcher Dick Selma), and a secretary
named Lou Blatz, who is 71 years old and who in 1916 pitched
for the Chicago Whales of the Federal League on a diamond
that would eventually become Wrigley Field.

Before April ends the Cardinals visit Wrigley Field, defeat
the Cubs in a single game, and depart trailing by just 4½.
"The next time we leave Chicago," states Red Schoendienst,
their manager, "we'll be in first place."

The Cubs, of course, have different plans, which are
reflected a week later in Philadelphia. There they learn that
the Detroit Tigers will follow them into town for an exhibition

game, and so one of them scrawls a message on the black-board for the defending world champions. "See you in the World Series," it says, "if you can make it."

The fever grows, blossoms, transforms itself into hysteria, and when the Cubs return from their first lengthy trip, they're greeted at the airport by adulating masses. Ernie Banks is now a Sunday sports reporter, Channel 9 is outdrawing its competition, and 600 calls and 2,000 letters a day are flooding the team's office, many of them requesting World Series tickets.

They frolic through May, and traipse through June, and beautiful Wrigley Field is a child's fantasyland.

A single, discordant note is sounded when a bitter Adolfo Phillips is shipped to Montreal after a public lashing by Durocher, but this can be ignored — there are celebrations to enjoy. Kessinger, Banks, Santo, Williams, Holtzman, and Jenkins are among the league leaders, and now Glenn Beckert is back, too, and blossoming at second after a staggering series of discomfitures. Kessinger breaks a record for consecutive errorless games in a season, and Williams breaks a record for consecutive games played. Santo is kicking his heels after each victory, and Dick Selma is waving his towel each day, exhorting those Bleacher Bums who need no enticement. Durocher marries for the fourth time, Banks begins writing a column for *The Tribune,* and finally the players hire an agent to help them parlay sudden success into cash. "I'm elated at the way this team is playing," Durocher chortles. "They smell the money."

On July 8 they travel to New York for a three-game series with the Mets, who are a fairy tale. These imps, these waifs, are now their closest pursuers, just five games behind, but no one on the Cubs believes in magic.

Through eight innings of this first game, they do just that, and they coast into the ninth leading 3–1. Ferguson Jenkins has been brilliant, merely nicked by Ed Kranepool's fifth-inning home run, and only the most fervent of Met worshippers believes a miracle possible.

Ken Boswell provides fodder for this dream by leading off

with a pop fly to short right-center that drops amidst Young and Kessinger and Beckert for a double. Tommie Agee fouls out to Banks, but then Donn Clendenon pinch hits and drives a ball toward deep left-center. Young, who froze on Boswell's hit, races after this one, reaches it, and grabs it, but then he slams into the wall and the ball falls from the webbing of his glove.

Cleon Jones follows with another double, driving in Boswell and Clendenon to tie the game, and then Ed Kranepool, the last of the original Mets, throws his bat at a pitch that has him fooled and loops a game-winning single just over Kessinger's head. "The Cubs went out there patting their pockets when they took the field in the ninth," Jones says. "They were already starting to count that twenty-five grand."

The Cubs, however, are only fuming, and Don Young is the object of their ire. He has dressed quickly and already escaped the locker room, but bitter words are still aimed at him. "He was just thinking of himself, not the team," snaps Santo. "He had a bad day at the bat, so he's got his head down. He's worrying about his batting average and not the team. All right, he can keep his head down, and he can keep right on going, out of sight for all I care. We don't need that kind of thing."

The next afternoon Santo calls a press conference in his 10th-floor room at the Waldorf Astoria and apologizes, but that night Young is on the bench and a rookie named Jim Qualls is in center field. More than 59,000 people are squeezed into Shea for this second game, and for 8⅓ innings they witness perfection, as Tom Seaver retires 25 men in a row. Then, with one out in the ninth, Jimmy Qualls, who is hitting but .243, pulls Seaver's first pitch into left-center to ruin the masterpiece.

Still, the Mets win 4–0. Moments before this series' last game begins, Ernie Banks says, "Look at them. They're calm for such a young team. That's pretty strange."

On this afternoon only the Mets' play is strange, and the Cubs take advantage of their multifarious errors and finally escape with a 6–2 victory. With that, Santo raises the gauntlet, and he departs New York with a warning: "Wait'll we get 'em in Wrigley Field next week."

The First Day of the Mets' visit is July 14, and by 6 o'clock that morning 15 Andy Frain ushers are at Wrigley Field to control the earliest arrivals. By 9:30, a half-hour before the parks open, there are 200 more of them, and for the game itself the police add 28 extra patrolmen and 3 sergeants.

There is no mistaking the rivalry now, and a pennant race and crazed fans and a pair of strong-willed teams are thrown together in a smoldering cauldron. On this afternoon, they produce a classic, and when it ends Bill Hands and the Cubs have defeated Tom Seaver and the Mets 1–0. Ron Santo dances his jig not once but many times, and the Bleacher Bums, unusually subdued during the game, are suddenly roaring. "ABEEBEE! UNGOWA! CUB POWUH!" they chant, copying a cheer that originally belonged to the Black Panthers.

"Yes, sir," says Leo Durocher in the locker room. "Yes, sir, that was a World Series game."

In their locker room, the Mets are ignoring the game and instead concentrating on Santo's antics. "Bush," Coach Joe Pignatano labels them, and the next afternoon he calls out to Santo during pregame practice. "Watch!" he shouts, and then he mimics him. "Bush, that's real bush," he concludes.

Santo answers with a traditional obscene gesture, but moments later, when he is at home plate and exchanging lineups with Met Manager Gil Hodges, he has no reply. "Tell Piggy that the only reason I click my heels is because the fans will boo me if I don't," the Cub captain tries to explain.

"You remind me of someone," says the laconic Hodges. "You remind me of Tug McGraw. When he was young and immature and nervous, he used to jump up and down, too. He doesn't do it anymore."

Santo is silent and still staring when Hodges whirls and returns to the dugout, and he is silent, too, at game's end. The Mets have won, 5–4, and one of their heroes has been

Al Weis, who hit his first home run of the year, his second home run in four years, his fifth home run in his career. "Were you surprised when the ball went out today?" someone asks Weis himself.

"I'm always surprised," says Weis.

The final Met surprise arrives in the final game of this series, and they knock out Jenkins after one batter in the second, exult over another of Weis' rare home runs, and win 9–5. Tom Seaver, normally all business, is one of the first out of his team's dugout after the victory is secured, and when he crosses the first-base line he stops, dances, then rises into the air and clicks his heels.

Ron Santo is not doing that. He is dazed, and in the locker room he sits for long moments with his feet propped onto a box filled with fan mail. "The Mets beat us," he finally says. "They beat us. You have to give them credit for that. Two out of three in our park. I still don't believe it."

That dream is still viable, despite the surprising Mets, and the Cubs sweep seven straight in early August, and they soar on the 19th, when Ken Holtzman pitches a no-hitter against the Braves. Philip Wrigley has already promised to double whatever shares his players might receive for appearing in the World Series, and two club executives have already traveled to Boston, to learn how a team with a small and ancient park handles that classic.

The Cubs even receive some help from the Mets, who, on August 13, fall 9½ behind and out of second place for the first time in 71 days.

Now, inexplicably, the lead begins to unravel. The Cubs lose three straight after Holtzman's triumph, then win two, then drop four more.

On August 26 the Cubs receive permission to print playoff tickets, yet the next day the Mets creep to within two games, the closest anyone has been since May 10. Then the team revives and enters September with a six-game winning streak.

But then the Pirates come into Wrigley and blast Holtzman

and Jenkins, and they then capture a third game with two unearned runs in the 11th following an error by Kessinger. The lead is 2½ and they must travel to Shea to face the torrid Mets.

Durocher is inflamed, and before the Cubs leave for New York, he berates them in the locker room. It does no good and on Monday night, September 8, they lose to the Mets 3–2, and then sit silently in their clubhouse.

They are in front by even less at the end of the next evening, for they are again defeated, this time 7–1. "Oh, this is wonderful," exults Met owner Joan Payson in her team's locker room.

The next night they face the Phillies, lose their seventh straight, drop out of first place, then wait for 15 minutes behind closed doors. When they are finally opened, Durocher says nothing, though Ron Santo states, "I'm optimistic, very optimistic."

They are defeated again the following night when the Phils score three in the eighth, then they move to St. Louis, where they beat the Cards before losing twice.

They're 3½ behind when they stagger into Montreal, then 4½ behind when they lose once more. "Sure we're pressing," Don Kessinger admits. "We wouldn't be human if we weren't. It's a human reaction."

They beat the Expos, return home, defeat the Phillies, and Santo declares, "I think I'm going to have an ulcer before this season is over." They lose to the Phillies, and Durocher declares, "It's far from over." They split with the Cardinals, and St. Louis reliever Jim Grant declares, "The monkey's tail ain't long now, and it's not as short as it's gonna be."

They lose again to the Cards, then defeat the Cards, then lose to the Expos on the day the Mets clinch the pennant and their own season-ticket holders receive order forms for playoff tickets. The next day, in front of 2,217, they beat the Expos, but it's over when the Mets also win. In the locker room a Chicago writer spots a New York writer. "What are you doing here?" the former asks.

"I'm here for the burial," the latter replies.

The following day John Lindsay, the mayor of New York, sends a telegram to Richard Daley, the mayor of Chicago. "I guess you know there is a pretty hot election going on here," the message reads. "However, Controller (Mario) Procaccino, State Sen. (John) Marchi and I absolutely agree on one thing — when it comes to baseball, Chicago is still the second city."

Roger Angell

Excerpt from Tiger, Tiger

Season Ticket

Early on the day of the first Cubs–Padres playoff game, Jim Frey went to his bedroom window to check the wind — *too* early, it turned out, for it was four-thirty in the morning and still pitch-black out there. He went back to bed. He got what he wanted, though, for there was a lovely Cubs wind at Wrigley Field by game time that afternoon — blowing straight out, that is, at a good twenty miles an hour — and throughout the day you could hear the shuffle and pop of the flags snapping in the breeze. The scoops of bunting set around the gray-blue facing of the steep upper deck were also astir, and, farther out, the tall center-field flagpole above the great gray-green scoreboard and the rising pyramid of bleachers flew a double row of pennants (team flags, in the order of finish, top to bottom, of the National League divisions), which kept up a gala, regattalike flutter all through the shining afternoon. The famous ivy, thickly overgrowing the outfield walls from pole to pole, showed October tints, and the graceful old brickwork of the inner-field facade suggested football weather as well. There were treetops swaying out along Waveland Avenue, beyond left field, and Sheffield Avenue, beyond right, and other flags were aloft on the rooftops of the low neighborhood houses there, with a fine range of colors and loyalties to choose among: Old Glory, Israel, Ireland, Puerto Rico, and, of course, the Cubs. In among the flags, a couple of

big tethered balloons shifted and shouldered in the moving
air, and the parapets and extemporaneous stands on the roofs
were jammed with unticketed, opportunistic fans, who counted
themselves lucky to be close enough to pick up glimpses of
the game along with the sounds and sense of it. The angling,
early-autumn sunlight illuminated white-and-blue Cubs pennants in the stands around the park and silhouetted a long,
sweeping line of heads and shoulders of the spectators in the
topmost row of the lower deck, and when the Cubs' center
fielder, Bob Dernier, sprinted to his left and abruptly bent
low to pull in a line drive, early on, there was a sudden gleam,
a dart of light, from his dark glasses as he made the grab.
Even the noises of the day — the deep, happy roaring of the
fans; the ancient, carny-show strains of the Wrigley Field
organ (sometimes playing upbeat old airs like Cole Porter's
"From This Moment On") — seemed to reach us with a washed
and wonderful clarity, and in my seat in the airy, down-sloping
lower left-field stands (an overflow press sector), I kept tight
hold on my rustling scorecard and stat sheets, and felt at one
with the weather and the world. It was as if the entire baseball season — all those hundreds of games and thousands of
innings — had happened, just this one time, in order to bring
this afternoon to pass: a championship game and the Cubs,
for once, in it. Only one possibility could spoil things on a day
like this — and I could almost see the same thought on the
faces of the holiday throngs pushing along under the stands
before game time: the unexpected, awful shadow of a doubt —
and even that was taken care of in the quickest possible way.
Dernier, leading off against the Padres' Eric Show in the
bottom of the first, rocketed the second pitch to him into the
screen above the left-field bleachers, and a bare moment or
two later Gary Matthews got another shot up into the wind,
which landed above and beyond the ivy in left center, a good
four hundred feet away. Rick Sutcliffe came up to bat in the
third, and *his* homer — a low, hurrying, near line drive over
the right-side bleachers: a *shot* — didn't need the wind at all,
and it told us, if any doubt remained, what kind of day this
was meant to be. Chicago won, 13–0.

Before we say goodbye to the Cubs, who are about to make their sudden departure from this season and this account (they won again the next afternoon, this time playing shortball — speed and defense and the extra base — for a neat 4–2 decision), another lingering look at the Friendly Confines and its team may be forgiven. The Cubs' great success in 1984 and their abrupt termination in the championships can be best appreciated if we remind ourselves about the team's unique place in the sport. The Cubs are the Smithsonian of baseball, a caucus of institutions, many of which were on view during the playoff festivities. "Mr. Cub," Ernie Banks, who put in nineteen years' distinguished service at shortstop and first base, reappeared in uniform as an honorary member of the 1984 team and threw out the first ball (a trick flip from behind his back on the mound) before the first game. The next day, the ritual was performed by Jack Brickhouse, who had broadcast thirty-four years of Cub games before his retirement, in 1982; his successor in the booth, the incumbent Harry Caray, is a *transferred* institution, who had previously put in eleven years' work with the White Sox. Bill Veeck, who sat in the center-field bleachers throughout the season and the playoffs (I spotted him there through my binoculars, with a Vincent van Gogh straw hat on his bean, a beer in his hand, and his pegleg comfortably out in the aisle while a stream of friends and writers and well-wishers came by to shake his hand and spoil his view)* was most recently in baseball as the owner and chief executive of the White Sox, but his father, William Veeck, Sr., was president of the Cubs from 1919 to 1933, and Veeck the Younger grew up in Wrigley Field and had his first job in the business with the team

---

*I almost walked out there to pay my respects to Veeck, a favorite old friend of mine, but then I decided that I didn't want to add to the distracting crush of admirers around him. So many reporters wanted to interview him during the playoffs that he was forced to set up a schedule of incoming telephone interviews at his house; one writer told me he had got his story at seventwenty in the morning. Bill Veeck died fifteen months later, but I treasure this distant last glimpse of him at home in his favorite old ballpark and relishing a game. Baseball, he always said, should be *savored.*

thereafter. It was Bill Veeck, in fact, who persuaded the Wrigleys to plant ivy out along the outfield walls, in 1938. Steve Trout, the southpaw who pitched and won the second playoff game against the Padres, is a son of Dizzy Trout, who pitched and won a game against the Cubs in their last previous postseason adventure, the 1945 World Series, against Detroit. And so on. The best-known Cub fixture, of course — almost an honored institution — is defeat. No other club has had a manager who described his team's home fans as unemployables, as did a recent incumbent named Lee Elia, and no other franchise has taken so mild a view of its own fortunes as to allow its team to amble along with no manager at all, as the Cubs did from 1961 to 1965, when the day-to-day direction was handled by a rotating board of coaches. Leo Durocher took over after that and whipped the team up into second place a couple of times, but the last pennant, in '45, is still so vivid in the memory of the fans that this year in Chicago I kept hearing references to Hank Borowy, the pitcher who won the first and sixth games of that World Series, and lost the fifth and seventh.

We won't know for some time where the 1984 Cubs will fit into this sweet, dismal history, but I think we can already do honor to the principals — Dallas Green and Jim Frey, and the newborn or newbought stars on the field — for reversing this deep-running tide so precipitately. There was no preparation for this at the beginning of the year, when the Cubs, fifth-place finishers the year before, lost eleven straight games in spring training, but some late trades suddenly filled the team's needs — a leadoff man, a center fielder, more speed (Bob Dernier, who came from the Phillies on March 27th, took care of all three), more and then still more pitching — and they began to win and began to be noticed. On June 23rd, before a national television audience, the Cubs beat the Cardinals, 12–11, in eleven innings, in a game in which Ryne Sandberg, their remarkable young star, hit two home runs against Bruce Sutter — one in the ninth and another in the tenth (with two out and a man aboard), each

time retying the score. "Sandberg is the best player I have
ever seen," Cardinal manager Whitey Herzog said afterward.

It is the Cub fans who will have to sort out this season —
most of all, the unshirted, violently partisan multitudes in the
Wrigley Field bleachers, who sustain the closest fan-to-player
attachment anywhere in baseball — and I will not patronize
them by claiming a share of their happiness during the
summer or pretending to understand their pain and shock at
its end. Baseball, as I have sometimes suggested, is above all
a matter of belonging, and belonging to the Cubs takes a
lifetime. But to Chicago the Cubs are something more than
just a team. Wrigley Field is almost the last of the old
neighborhood ballparks, and the antiquity of the place (it was
built in 1914, two years after Fenway Park opened for
business in Boston) and the absence of night ball there (the
Wrigley family believed that the crowds and the noise would
be an affront to the nearby residents) remind us what the
game once felt like and how it fitted into the patterns of city
life. I took a little stroll around the blocks off to the north and
east of Wrigley Field one morning before game time and fell
into conversation with a short, cheerful young woman named
Debra Price, who was out jogging. She was wearing a
sweatshirt with huge Cubs emblazoning, and was accompanied by her black cat, Dufus, who runs with her. She told me
she had lived just around the corner, on Kenmore Avenue,
until August, when she took a job in Denver (she is in labor
relations), but had come back for the games because her old
roommate, Karen Miller, had been lucky enough to get a hold
of a pair of tickets. "I was going through a bad Cubs with-
drawal out there," she said. "It used to be incredibly conve-
nient living so close to the park here. You could walk over at
nine in the morning and pick up your seats for that afternoon.
It was always easy to get seats, because the team wasn't
going anywhere. I can't quite believe this whole year, or
understand it. I'm a little young to be a real Cubs fan, but I
think I qualify. I was there two years ago the day Bill Buckner
got his two-hundredth hit of the season, and Jody Davis has

been sort of a constant for me. There's a lot of character and
sentimentality in what the Cubs are. They've always seemed
older than the White Sox in this town — I don't know why.
They have this kind of *humor* about them. The Cubs are
outside the realm."

On Grace Street, I paid an impromptu visit to the House of
the Good Shepherd, a convent whose sizable, unmarked
back-yard parking lot has been a public secret shared by
suburban Cubs fans for forty years or more. The parking
revenue now accounts for more than a third of the annual
budget for the convent, which does its main work in family
care. I was told about this by a pleasant, impressive nun
named Sister Patricia, who said she respected and admired
the Cubs for sticking to daytime ball. She wouldn't quite
declare her own feelings about this year's team, but I thought
I could tell that she was — well, *pleased.* I asked about a
vendor I had seen out on Grace Street who was selling wonderful T-shirts with the message "THE CUBS — A TICKET
TO HEAVEN," but Sister Patricia shook her head. "Not ours,"
she said. "That's outside the walls." When I took my leave, I
noticed that the sister who let me out was wearing a little
paper Cubs logo — the red letter "C" inside a circle of blue —
over her heart on her white habit.

The side blocks off Grace Street were made up of elderly
detached three-story houses, with scraps of lawn and flower
beds out in front; the grass had a worn, late-summer look to
it, and the low-hanging tree branches were heavy with dusty
leaves. Here and there, the narrow concrete sidewalk had a
half-circle cut out, making room for a fat tree trunk. I could
have been in Keokuk or Kirksville, but whenever I crossed a
street I could look off to my left a couple of blocks and see the
great back wall of Wrigley Field. Down another street, Clifton
Avenue, I came upon a man named Barry Flanagan, who was
carefully brushing a fresh coat of green paint on his front
stoop. When I stopped to talk, we were joined by his father,
James Flanagan, a retired gent with a ruddy face and gold-
rimmed glasses. The senior Mr. Flanagan was born in

England — there was still a trace of that when he talked —
and used to root for the West Ham football team, but he took
up the other game when he came to the new country and the
Cubs' neighborhood. The Flanagans had been in the same
house for twenty-seven years, and before that they had lived
just next door. They were great Ernie Banks fans, of course.
They could *hear* the games, Barry told me, but couldn't quite
see them — not even from the roof. I had the feeling that
they didn't get around to going very often. "I can tell by the
people walking home after a game whether they've won or
lost," the elder Flanagan said. "When the Cubs lose, they're
saying, 'Oh, we should have done this, we should have done
that.' Some days, if there's been a bad game, they trample
the flowers a bit. But it's nice having the Cubs. You know
there's always going to be parking space right after the
games, when you're coming home from work."

I said goodbye and headed off for the park, and all along the
street I noticed yellow signs put up in the lower windows of
the little houses: "NO NIGHT BASEBALL" — a response to
the rumor, back in midsummer, that the postseason games in
Chicago might be played under some temporarily installed
floodlights in order to placate the demands of the networks
for night ball and its vast audiences and numbers. Now (it's
only to be expected, I suppose) Dallas Green is talking about
building a new ballpark somewhere for the Cubs, with more
seats, improved parking, and, of course, night baseball.

I watched the rest of the N.L. playoffs, out in San Diego,
by television: some fine pitching by Ed Whitson in the 7–1
Padre victory in Game Three; the riveting attacks and
ripostes of the next game, in which Steve Garvey again and
again surpassed himself — surpassed possibility, almost —
in the 7–5 Padre victory that tied things up; and some useful
work by the top two hitters in the San Diego lineup, Alan
Wiggins and Tony Gwynn, in the team's 6–3 comeback
victory over Rick Sutcliffe in the Sunday finale. Garvey, it will
be recalled, batted in the second San Diego run in Game Four
with a double; tied it with a single in his next at-bat; drove in

the go-ahead run in the seventh, and, with matters again tied, whacked the game-winning two-run line-drive homer in the ninth, against Lee Smith; five runs batted in for the day. Garvey has his detractors, who are put off at times by his smiling, TV-host persona, but I am not among them; I was startled by his great day at the plate, but not surprised. What I can't decide, even at this distance, is whether Jim Frey should have taken out Rick Sutcliffe, his star and stopper, much sooner in the final game, when he proved unable to hold a three-run lead. To be sure, Sutcliffe had often found himself in similarly horrid places during the summer, as all pitchers do, and had pitched out of them, but even in the middle innings of this game, before the Padres had been able to put anything together at the plate, he had looked uncharacteristically uncertain and unhappy out there — an amazing and disconcerting sight. The pressure of such a too short series is killing, of course, and a deepening and palpable weight and doubt about the outcome of this last game had begun to swing against the Cubs well before it began. It's second-guessing, but I would have pitched Sutcliffe on Saturday.

The Padre fans, it will be recalled, kept up an unending, unquenchably ferocious din through all those games at San Diego's Jack Murphy Stadium. They actually seemed to make a difference, and thus had some part in the great comeback — all the Padre players said so at the end — but I must confess that I resented them a little, once their team had triumphed. The Padres had not come close in their fifteen years of campaigning, never finishing above fourth place, and I did not think that their supporters quite understood the kind of waiting and the hope and pain that Cub fans know by heart. Now, to be sure — since the playoffs, I mean — the Padres have been in a World Series and lost it, which changes everything. Their fans have won and *then* lost, and they are in the game at last.

THE FRIENDLY CONFINES

The Yankees have their 33 pennants, their pinstripes, and the Babe. The Red Sox have their Fenway Franks and their Green Monster. The Cardinals have their Clydesdales, the Royals their Dancing Waters, and the Padres their Chicken. And just about every team in the majors can lay claim to greater on-the-field success than the Cubs over the past four decades. But nobody, meaning nobody, has got what we've got: the best damn ballpark that ever was or ever will be, period. Anyone who questions why otherwise self-respecting persons would devote themselves to a team that considers .500 ball a successful season need only spend an afternoon — or, yes, an evening — amidst the ivy, brick, and green grass of Wrigley Field to understand why the Cubs retain their special place in the hearts of Chicagoans. It's a kind of magic that fans could never hope to experience in places like, say, Toronto's retractable dome. The Friendly Confines are the crowning glory of the Cubs' appeal, and our collection would not be complete without a bit of literary rumination on our own Field of Dreams.

Though E. M. Swift wrote his essay B.L. (Before Lights), his comprehensive anecdotal history of Wrigley Field reminds us that the park is defined, above all, by its luminous (no pun intended) traditions. Next baseball maverick Bill Veeck tells how he started cutting his nonconformist image working for the Cubs front office. An inevitable by-product of tradition is, of course, nostalgia, and David Broder and Joe Mantegna share a few personal sentiments born of childhood afternoons spent at Wrigley. Finally, we offer up some varying and esteemed thoughts on the latest chapter of our stadium's saga, the Great War of the Lights. First, Bernie Lincicome and George Will proffer dueling attitudes on the advisability of night ball at Wrigley; then Tom Callahan reports on that certain glowing event of 8/8/88, rounding out the proceedings with a few thoughts on what it all may — or may not — mean.

E. M. Swift

One Place That Hasn't
Seen the Light

Sports Illustrated, July 7, 1980

Wrigley Field is a ball *park*. If there was one way to rile Philip
K. Wrigley, the retiring gentleman who owned the Chicago
Cubs between 1932 and his death in 1977, it was to refer to
Wrigley Field as a stadium. It is a park, with spiders and
grasshoppers and vines an inch around on the field of play.
The vines come into bloom in mid-May. The morning glories
open up pale blue and pink and purple and are shut again by
noon. The greenish-white flowers of the bittersweet bloom
inconspicuously against the ivy. There is Boston ivy with its
eight-inch leaves that stick out from the brick a foot and a
half and are clipped by the ground crew before every home
stand. There is Baltic ivy with its shiny, leathery leaves that
stay green all winter, and the high-climbing Virginia creeper,
whose five-leaflet clusters turn reddish-orange in the fall.
That is when the bunches of grapes hang purple on the
grapevines and the bittersweet berries turn red, but in the
spring there are flowers where the fruit will be.

It is a park built for baseball. There are older ball parks —
Comiskey, right across town, is one — and stadiums both
bigger and smaller. But none can match Wrigley for watching
a baseball game; the $1.50 seats in the leftfield bleachers are
better than most stadiums' upperdeck boxes. People may

talk about that "quaint little bandbox" of a ball park in Boston, but there is nothing quaint about the new electronic message-board the size of centerfield, and anyone who has ever watched a game in the bleacher seats beneath that message-board would take issue with calling Fenway Park "little." You can sit fully 600 feet from home plate.

Wrigley Field is a classic Midwestern cross between penurious efficiency and charm. Its slightly off-kilter center-field scoreboard is the last in the majors still operated by hand, yet it is the only one that gives inning-by-inning scores of all out-of-town games. The roof is held up by a rusted network of rafters, a maze of horizontals and verticals and diagonals. Wrigley Field is a Peter Pan of a ball park. It has never grown up and it has never grown old. Let the world race on — they'll still be playing day baseball in the friendly confines of Wrigley Field, outfielders will still leap up against the vines, and the Cubs . . . well, it's the season of hope. This could be the Cubbies' year.

There is a tendency to credit the atmosphere in Wrigley Field to Philip K. Wrigley's traditional approach to the game, but evidence points to other forces at work. Mr. Wrigley was more innovator than traditionalist. In 1968, when synthetic turf was being developed, Wrigley was one of the first owners in baseball to look into digging up his park's natural sod and replacing it with artificial grass. It was only his inherent frugality that prevented him from going ahead with it. "When we have the money we'll probably install synthetic grass," Wrigley said. "There's no doubt it would pay for itself in a few years." One year he instituted a rotating system of head coaches instead of a single manager, an experiment ridiculed by the baseball Establishment. The Cubs were the first — and are now the only — team to televise every home game. Wrigley Field was the first ball park to install an organ, the first to have a Ladies Day.

White Sox owner Bill Veeck writes in his autobiography: "Old men, playing dominoes across the hearth, like to say that Phil Wrigley was the last of the true baseball men because he is the only owner who still holds, in the simple faith of his ancestors, that baseball was meant to be played under God's own sunlight. I know better. Having blown the chance to be first with lights, Mr. Wrigley just wasn't going to do it at all."

In fact, Wrigley Field was all set to be outfitted with lights in late 1941. The Cincinnati Reds had introduced night baseball in 1935, so it was still a relatively new attraction, and President Roosevelt thought it would be a good way to give factory workers some relaxation at night. The lights had been paid for and were on the verge of being installed when fate intervened in the form of Pearl Harbor. On Monday, December 8, the Cubs offered their towers, lights and cables to the U.S. Government, and they were used in the suddenly booming shipyards.

Right up through the '60s there was talk of installing lights in Wrigley Field so the Chicago Bears could start their football games later in the day and the Cubs could finish games that otherwise would be called on account of darkness. But the Bears moved to Soldier Field, and Wrigley Field remained unchanged.

"We can still draw without night games," say E.R. (Salty) Saltwell, vice-president of park operations. "We're not in this to lose money or break even. We draw heavily from young college, high school and junior high school kids during the summer, mainly because we have all day games."

Last year, with an 80–82 record that left them fifth in their division, the Cubs — with all their home games televised — nevertheless drew 1,648,587 fans. They come back like old lovers, by bus and via the El. They do not drive. There is not enough parking in the vicinity of the park to drive, which is another reason for the day games. They come back, and at worst they have an afternoon in the sunshine in the park, watching men at play and remembering what it was like when their fathers took them. What *they* were like. At best, the Cubs win. "If you can just play .500 ball for these fans they are happy," ex–Cub Manager Herman Franks said near the end of last season, the day he announced his retirement. "Can you imagine what they'd be like if you ever won a pennant for them?"

They would probably become crabby. Baseball fans spoil easily. The Cubs' last pennant was in 1945 (they have never even won a division title), and that 35-year drought is the driest spell in the major leagues. One of the reasons Cub fans are equable if their team finishes at .500 or better is that in the 20 seasons between 1947 and 1966 it did so only twice. In 1952 the Cubs went 77–77; in 1963, 82–80 — rebounding from a 1962 season unnerving to the staunchest of Cub fans, when the record was 59–103, and Chicago finished six games behind the Houston Colts, an expansion team.

Franks added, sounding like God speaking to the Israelites, "I know it's a terrible thing to ask, but you've got to have patience. The team is still two or three years away."

One of the silliest but most widespread fallacies in baseball is that Wrigley Field is somehow responsible for the Cubs' difficulties. That playing baseball games outdoors in the summer sun will, by August, sap a professional athlete of his strength. This theory would be more acceptable if they were the Sahara Cubs and each player was stripped and bound in the sand before his turn at bat, but 2½ hours in the Chicago sun — half of which is spent in the dugout — could not seriously tax a fat albino.

It has also been suggested that the way the ball flies into Waveland Avenue when the wind is blowing out so shatters the confidence of Cubs pitchers that they never recover. (At 368 feet, the power alleys in Wrigley Field are the shortest in baseball, and it was once 38 years between no-hitters there.) This, at least, is possible — Fergie Jenkins is the only Cub starter ever to win the Cy Young Award.

But to those who follow the team with even casual interest the real problem is simple. Talent. The Cubs either lack speed, power, pitching or defense, year after year. Often they lack all of the above. When they get a young Lou Brock, they trade him for an Ernie Broglio. Why blame the ball park for a trade like that? Cabdriver Harold Wolfson speaks for most Chicagoans when he says, "The Wrigleys are cheapos. They're all cheapos. Whenever anybody wanted money they traded him."

Papa Carl Leone was born the last year the Cubs won the World Series, 1908. He has only one tooth left that is visible, and he has only one eye. The other eye, he says, he lost to a line drive during batting practice. The teeth he just lost. Papa Carl has been coming to Wrigley Field since the year the Cubs moved there, 1916. He sits in the rightfield bleachers — the dean of "Bleacher Bums."

Wrigley Field was actually built in 1914 by a man named "Lucky Charlie" Weeghman. He owned the Chicago Whales of the short-lived Federal League, which lasted four seasons, 1912–15. The park, then called Weeghman Park, was completed in time for the 1914 opener at a cost of $250,000, and it seated 14,000 fans. When the American and National Leagues absorbed the Federal League in 1916, part of the deal was that Weeghman could buy the Chicago Cubs, who were then owned by Charles Taft of Cincinnati, brother of the former President. He did so for $500,000, putting together a syndicate of 10 investors, one of whom was the chewing-gum magnate, William Wrigley, Jr. By December of 1918, Wrigley had become the majority stockholder, Lucky Charlie had resigned, and Weeghman Park had become Cubs park. It was renamed Wrigley Field in 1926 when construction was started on the upper deck.

There were no permanent bleachers then. Temporary bleachers had been put into leftfield in 1923 to aid a strongman named Hack Miller, who, during the 1922 season, hit 12 home runs but had many other fly balls caught near the fence. It was said that Miller, who was 5'9", 195, could push a tenpenny nail through a board two inches thick with his bare hands, though if this were true one wonders why the fences had to be pulled in to help him hit home runs. In 1923, with bleachers installed in front of what had been the wall, Miller hit 20 homers, his career high. In 1924 he hit four and in '25 he hit two. The bleachers — and Miller — were removed posthaste, since the Cub pitchers were, in the meantime, getting shellacked.

In the next few years, when Hack Wilson arrived and the Cubs started to win, fans were allowed to watch the game behind a rope in the outfield when there were overflow crowds — Neanderthal versions of what are now the Bleacher Bums. "When the Cubs were up," recalls Papa Carl, "we'd all step forward and pull the rope up. When the other team was up and hit one deep, we'd pull it back and let the guy catch it."

This sort of fan participation became impossible in the 1929 and 1932 World Series, however, when the Cubs erected bleachers on the sidewalks outside the ball park in left- and rightfields. The centerfield bleachers were already permanently in place, of course, and it was in their direction that Babe Ruth "called his shot," his final World Series home run. There has always been some question as to whether Ruth, in fact, *did* call his shot, and to whom, or for whom, he was pointing. The Bleacher Bum version is that he was pointing to a black man named Amos (Loudmouth) Latimer, traveling secretary for the Chicago Negro League's 47th Street team. The story, which Loudmouth told for years afterward on 47th Street, goes that Latimer had been provoking Ruth from the centerfield bleachers by throwing lemon rinds at him and calling him "brother," a reference Ruth had heard before because of his facial features and the fact that he was an orphan. Ruth finally turned around and, from the field, told Loudmouth he had one coming. The next inning he deposited Charlie Root's delivery a few feet away from Amos. The Yankees, of course, won the Series.

There was an Andy Frain usher at the game named Leo Jonas, who was fresh out of grammar school and working his first Series. Jonas is now the senior Andy Frain at the park, having worked every baseball game in Wrigley Field since 1945. At night he Andy Frains at the harness track, and in the winter he works conventions at McCormick Place and the

Shrine Circus and has a two-week "vacation" at Christmas-time working crowd control for Marshall Field's Santa Claus. He is 65. "I'll retire when I won't be able to walk around," Jonas says. "No Social Security for me. I won't even apply for it; throw the letters right in the trash. I just miss it when I leave here at the end of the season. I can't wait for the spring to roll around. I like being outside in the sun and fresh air. The years went by so fast I don't even feel it."

It is the Peter Pan syndrome. Wrigley Field has kept him young. He still uses public transportation to get to the park — Belmont bus to Clark, Fullerton bus to the El, El to the Addison stop and two blocks to the rightfield-bleachers gate that he works — a route he would not care to take if there were night games. "A little rougher crowd would come in at night," he says. Old Andy Frain himself used to come into the Jonas family's variety store to buy cigars — Perfecto Garcias. They are another of Wrigley Field's charms — the Andy Frain ushers. They are generally accepted as the best in the business, polite, efficient and neat, men who will lead you to your seat and not accept a tip.

"I don't think the *fans* have changed too much," says Jonas. "The players have. You could watch those old guys play ball forever. They were so interesting. Hack Wilson was a little pudgy guy who looked like one of the kids on the playground. But he sure swung that bat, and away it went. Then he'd run around the bases like a little duck.

"Wilson and Pat Malone used to stay out till two or three partying, then the next day they came to the park early, and the manager, Joe McCarthy, would hit them fly balls to sweat the liquor out of them. It would be 80° in the park, and 90° on the field. But they played. Those writers say they fold up now because they play all day games. Look at all the pennants they won before. Players weren't swooning all over the field saying, 'I'm too hot, I can't play.' If you're an athlete . . ." Jonas does not need to complete the thought. Just then the old peanut man walks by. "Irving," Jonas asks, "how long you been here?"

"I just got here," Irving says. The game has not started yet.

"No. How many years?"

"Thirty years. *Peanuts!*" Irving would have difficulty eating a peanut, because he has no teeth.

"You're not thinking of retiring, are you?" Jonas asks.

"No," Irving says, thinking about it. He takes off his paper cap and wipes his white hair off his forehead. "I might drop dead." There is that option. "Or my wife might kill me." And that one. But retirement? From Wrigley Field? *"Peanuts!"* And he is gone.

The ballpark assumed its present configuration in 1937, when the bleachers were added in leftfield and the centerfield scoreboard was modernized, a step that included the removal of the Doublemint Twins from its crest. Since then there has been no advertising in the park.

It was at that time that Veeck, an employee of Phil Wrigley's in his youth, suggested planting the ivy. "Can't say it was original," says Veeck. "There was ivy on the wall at old Perry Field in Indianapolis." When Wrigley gave him the go-ahead, Veeck had copper wire strung from the brick walls so the ivy and bittersweet, a thousand plants in all, would have something to climb on. That copper wire, tarnished green, has long since been pulled from the brick by the vines it once supported and is suspended in a hopeless tangle among the berries and grapes and spider webs. In the meantime, the ivy has not only thrived on the field, but is one of the hottest concession items the Cubs handle. Last year the 2,500 plants — cuttings of outfield ivy potted up — put on sale for $1.50 each were a complete sellout.

The man who has taken care of those vines for the last 40 years is Roy (Cotton) Bogren, a short, silent Swede who started working in the clubhouse in 1936 and moved to the ground crew four years later. In 1957 he was made assistant and in 1970 was named ground superintendent. The vines are trimmed before every home stand. The Merion bluegrass field is mowed every third day during the spring, every fifth or sixth day after that, to a height that varies between 1½ and two inches. The infield is cut with hand mowers, and the clippings are allowed to fall. It is cut at night. Every third day it is watered, and four or five times a year the grass is fertilized with Scotts Plus Two, which controls weeds. The mound and home plate are clay, and the dirt of the infield is three parts loam to one part bank sand, which is a very fine sand.

The 22-man ground crew is also responsible for cleaning up the stands. Many of the seats in Wrigley Field still have to be raised by hand, and in 1925, when Bogren was a boy growing up two blocks from Wrigley Field — then Cubs Park — he would get out of school at 3:15 and, if it was a game day, head to the ball park, where the ground superintendent let him and his friends raise seats for a free pass to the next game. It is a practice that has continued. Bogren has given out as many as 50 passes to kids when there has been a big crowd, letting them in to race down the aisles, flipping up seats and dreaming about one day playing in that park — half an hour of work for a pass. So it is that Cub fans are made, diehard fans, fans that come back, win or lose. It is a ball park run by people.

Bogren used to work inside the scoreboard, another job for the ground crew, and one that requires three men, one for each level. Every so often an opposing team accuses the Cubs of stealing signs from inside that scoreboard, but if that has ever been the purpose the crew has never been very good at it. There is only one entrance into the scoreboard, and that is by ladder from the top of the bleachers in center. It is a huge, dark, musty structure, with ladders between levels and a ticker tape on which the scores of other games are received. The scoreboard numbers are metal and they are fitted into slats at the completion of an inning. There is a phone to the press box in case the ticker-tape machine breaks, or someone inadvertently puts a number in upside down. Between 1942 and '62 Bogren worked there, and it is not with fondness that he recalls it.

"It often gets so hot in the summertime you can't believe it," he says. "The worst days were when the wind was coming off the lake, from the back. We didn't have any holes in the back. It's probably gotten better now. It's rusted through in places, but that still doesn't count as ventilation."

Bogren rummages through a stack of old football numbers lying around the floor of the scoreboard structure, numbers like 42, which, in Wrigley Field, might someday be used for a baseball game. There is a VENEZUELA from the 1959 Pan Am Games. There is no bathroom. Bogren is asked about this, since no one is allowed in or out during the game.

"Right there," he says. "That old copper funnel." There is a pipe coming up out of the floor that leads heaven knows where, with a copper funnel at the top. "Same one that's been there since 1937," Bogren says. "Shows you how good copper is."

Papa Carl Leone has written the names of his "boys" on the seats of the rightfield bleachers so that no one else will accidentally sit in them before the game. His "boys" are not sitting in them before the game because they are waiting outside for batting-practice home runs to rain down on Waveland Avenue. One fellow named Rich has caught 700. Last season Atlanta was the favorite visiting club, hitting 27 balls out before one game. Most of the ball hounds pay their way inside the park after batting practice is over, but three or four diehards wait in the streets all game, playing stickball or throwing a football while listening to the radio broadcast, stopping completely only when Dave Kingman comes to bat. Kenmore Street runs perpendicular to Waveland, and a third of the way down the block an X is painted on the sidewalk where Kong's longest shot landed, 533 feet from home plate.

On the corner of Waveland and Sheffield, a block from the El, is Ray's Bleachers, meeting place for the hard-core, hard-hatted Wrigley Field Bleacher Bums who terrorized opposing leftfielders in 1969–70–71, when the Cubs made respectable pennant runs only to collapse in August and September. There is a poster of Ron (Pizza) Santo on the wall and

countless other bits of Cub memorabilia. The Bleacher Bums'
behavior was so inciteful that in 1970 the Cub management installed a 42-inch chain-link fence around the top of
the outfield wall to discourage fan participation. When Leo
Durocher was manager from 1966–1972, he declared Ray's
Bleachers off limits for the Cubs — but Dick Selma and
Fergie Jenkins regularly disregarded this edict, in the proud
tradition of Hack Wilson and Pat Malone. Selma used to lead
the Bums in cheers from the bullpen and became so popular
that when he was traded to the Phillies and came back to play
a game, the bleacher crowd showered him with quarters.
Selma ran out with a satchel and, after the game, brought all
the change to Ray's, putting the satchel on the bar and
declaring the drinks were on him until the quarters ran out.

"They deserve a pennant," says Ray Meyer, proprietor of
Ray's Bleachers.

About 80 of the original Bums still return regularly, and last
year one held his baby shower at Ray's. "It's the same story
every year," says Meyer. "It gets sad near the end."

It gets sad near the end because it is the end of another
season, not because it is the end of another pennantless
season. If you think about it for long, it becomes very sad, so
you don't. So you just go on, like Papa Carl, who, the last day
of the last season, took four weepy young bleacher ladies
who would not see him again until spring and hugged them to
his brown, wrinkled chest. The bleachers are the only place
in Wrigley Field where males may remove their shirts, which,
of course, is why Papa Carl sits there. As the girls said their
goodbys, Papa Carl winked his good eye and grinned, expos-
ing his one good tooth, "How'm I doin'?" he said. "Pretty
good, eh?"

Bill Veeck with Ed Linn

The Battle of Wrigley Field

Veeck as in Wreck

From a purely financial standpoint my father's death, coming as it did in the midst of the Depression, could not have occurred at a worse time. We had lived well. Now his investments, like everybody else's, had gone sour. I returned to Kenyon to finish out the football season, then went to the Cubs' office and asked for a job. William Wrigley had died two years earlier. Phil Wrigley, his son, hired me as office boy at $18 a week.

That was all right. In the eight years I remained with the Cubs, I received a sound and solid education in every phase of a baseball club's table of organization. The same week I went to work for the Cubs, I began to work the switchboard for the Chicago Bears who, of course, played their football games at Wrigley Field. During the winter, I worked on the ground crew. The next winter, Mr. Wrigley got me a job at the Cubs' advertising agency and he soon had me putting out a magazine — and a pretty good one — to be sent to Cub fans.

I ran the commissary and I worked with the ushers. I worked the ticket windows and the ticket office. I ran the tryout school for high school players. I was in charge of park maintenance at the time Wrigley Field was being rebuilt and, at the end, I was the club treasurer and assistant secretary. Turn my wallet upside down and union cards will come tumbling out.

To everything, there is a craft. Take tickets. George Doyle, the head of our ticket department, not only taught me the tricks of the trade, he got me jobs in arenas and theatres all over town. I like to think that I can still count tickets fast enough to get a job anywhere in the country. A professional, working under pressure, picks up a whole block of tickets and riffles them alongside his ear, like a gambler counting a deck. After a great deal of experience, you know through a combination of the sound and the feel exactly where to stop. And you have to be accurate; close doesn't count. When Doyle requested that the front office send me down to check the ticket windows during the 1935 World Series, I felt highly honored; each ticket, representing three home games, was worth $39.60.

Concessions are a whole little world in themselves, a world that has continued to fascinate me. You would be amazed how much sheer psychology is involved in selling a hot dog and beer. In designing the new concession stands at Wrigley Field, I wanted to install fluorescent lighting. I was told that fluorescent lighting could not be used outdoors because, as everyone knew, the lights wouldn't work in the cold. Well, baseball isn't exactly a winter sport. I told them to put in the fluorescents anyway and we'd see what happened. What happened was the lights worked fine (they also worked fine during the football season and would presumably work splendidly in any well-appointed igloo).

What also happened was that our business immediately fell off drastically. I had the mistake — in the luck of the draw — of choosing a hard blue-white fluorescent, a lighting particularly cruel to women. Women seem to be born with some tribal instinct about these things; they would not come to the stand no matter how hungry they were. We changed to a soft rose-white, which is flattering to women, and quickly picked up all the old business and more besides.

At the same time I learned something so elementary that it is generally ignored in baseball. Female customers are not the same as male ones.

By working in the concession stands myself, I had come to

understand the importance of space. In a baseball park, people run up to the concessions between innings or stop off briefly on their way out. I found that when I was able to get from the red hots to the beer and coffee without having to move, I would sell both the red hot and a drink. If I had to take but one step, the beverage sales would begin to drop. I was even able to reduce it to a precise formula. *One extra step costs you 10 percent of your gross.* I therefore designed the concession stands myself and have been designing my own ever since. An architect will draw you a beautiful stand. So beautiful and spacious that you'll go broke.

I was in a position to be designing stands and supervising construction only because of Boots Weber, the man who had replaced my father. My father left me a far more valuable and lasting legacy than money. He left me a good name. All my life I have run across old friends of his eager to show their affection for him by helping his son. Boots had been running Wrigley's Los Angeles franchise, a post to which my father had reappointed him, and as a way of showing his affection and admiration, Boots more or less adopted me.

It was Boots who sent me to night school to study the subjects that would be most valuable around a ball park. I went to Northwestern to study accounting and business law — which have been invaluable — and to the Lewis Institute for designing and blueprint reading.

With a couple of hours to kill every night before going to school, I'd stay around the office with Boots and try to be helpful. Before long, I was his assistant and we were running the club together.

Difficult as it may be to say how much one man can owe another, I owe more to Boots Weber than to anyone else. Years later in Cleveland, I found a bright, clean-cut young boy named Stanley McIlvaine working behind the press-room bar. I sent him to night school to take accounting and business law, and moved him into the office to work with us during the day. When he finished night school, I sent him to Zanesville, Ohio, to run our Class-D club. Stanley is still in baseball. Last year, he was general manager at Dallas. It was my way of thanking Boots, in the way I thought he'd like to be thanked.

I stayed on with the Cubs, after the first few years, only because of Boots. Life with Phil Wrigley was always a battle between the baseball men and the gum men. Boots and I had to stand back-to-back to protect each other from sudden attack.

It is hard to understand how a father and son can be as completely different as William and Phil Wrigley. The father, who practically invented chewing gum, was the last of the super salesmen, a man who made his name synonymous with his product. He was a well-upholstered, jovial man who liked people and knew what made them tick.

The son was one of those men who is difficult to describe in a quick few words. I always called him Mr. Wrigley when I worked for him, I still call him Mr. Wrigley when I see him, and half the time I even think of him as Mr. Wrigley.

As a young man he was quiet and introspective and always perfectly happy to be overshadowed by a dynamic father whom he worshiped. His father left the club to him personally rather than to the estate, the only direct bequest in his will, and so Phil Wrigley assumed the burden out of his sense of loyalty and duty. If he has any particular feeling for baseball, any real liking for it, he has disguised it magnificently.

The one point on which we clashed, perennially, was promotion. I wanted it. He didn't. He was the boss. He won every argument. Mr. Wrigley, as a shy man, isn't interested in the press. It's more than that, though; he's a little afraid of writers. He sometimes leaves the impression he is afraid that if he opens himself up to them they'll compare him unfavorably with his father.

He isn't really a lesser man, he's just different. Let's have no misconceptions on this point, Mr. Phil Wrigley is a brilliant man. He has taken his father's company and built it into an international colossus, and don't give me any of that nonsense about it being easy for a son to step into an established enterprise. I have seen too many rich men's sons run their fathers' businesses into the ground. Mr. Wrigley would have been successful at anything he put his hand to. And that, in fact, is where he is happiest, putting his hands to things. He is a mechanical genius. His greatest relaxation is to strip an old automobile apart and put it back together.

He has invented several tools. One of his inventions, for example, is a screwdriver which slips into small openings and then is locked, by means of a lever, into the screw. But once he has built a prototype to prove to himself that it works, he loses all interest in it. The rights are given over to his mechanic.

A more honest and selfless man would be hard to find. While I was with the Cubs, he had an unbelievably altruistic working arrangement with Milwaukee. Wrigley did not believe in farm systems. It was his belief — and he was right — that baseball could only remain healthy if the minor league clubs were free to develop their own players and sell them to the highest bidder. He put his money where his mouth was. He subsidized Milwaukee, through a direct cash grant, and renounced all rights to their players. As a result, Whitlow Wyatt, the best pitcher in the minor leagues, was sold not to the Cubs but to the Dodgers. Two years later, Wyatt pitched the Dodgers to a pennant.

With all these virtues, Phil Wrigley has one overriding flaw. He knows more about things and less about people than any man I have ever met. In the eight years I worked for him, he almost never had a visit from a personal friend. He has few personal friends. Business associates, yes; friends, I don't know.

Because he is such a shy man, the associates he feels most comfortable with are not the ball-club employees — who are a gregarious, outspoken lot — but the gum company people. And so while he kept all my father's employees — the old group remained intact for 40 full years until death began to thin them out a couple of years ago — he also surrounded himself with a kitchen cabinet of gum executives who were always undercutting Boots and me.

Wrigley is one of those men who insists he despises yes-men. What he really means is that he wants you to talk a little before you agree with him. If you can reach *his* conclusion for your own reasons, so much the better. The gum men never gave him an argument about baseball. They couldn't. Eddie Gaedel knew more about baseball than most of them.

In the general area of promotion, Wrigley and I agree on only one thing: keeping the park clean. My father had always had a phobia about a clean park. Phil Wrigley carried it even further; he made the park itself his best promotion.

While he was doing it, he taught me perhaps the greatest single lesson of running a ball club. Wrigley compared the Cubs' won-and-lost records with corresponding daily-attendance charts and showed me that the two followed a practically identical pattern. His conclusion was inescapable. A team that isn't winning a pennant has to sell something in addition to its won-and-lost record to fill in those low points on the attendance chart. His solution was to sell "Beautiful Wrigley Field"; that is, to make the park itself so great an attraction that it would be thought of as a place to take the whole family for a delightful day. It was no accident that the title of the magazine I edited for him was *Fan and Family.*

Wrigley kept the park freshly painted. He threw out all the sidewalk vendors, newspaper boys and panhandlers. He stationed ushers out front to guide people to their sections. He insisted that the ticket sellers be polite and courteous.

We sold "Beautiful Wrigley Field." We advertised "Beautiful Wrigley Field." The announcers were instructed to use the phrase "Beautiful Wrigley Field" as often as possible. We sold it so well that when I came back to Chicago in 1959 as president of the White Sox, across town, I found "Beautiful Wrigley Field" my greatest single obstacle. Because "Beautiful Wrigley Field" tacitly implied "that run-down, crummy joint on the South Side."

By 1959, Wrigley was no longer keeping the park freshly painted. The neighborhood had deteriorated badly. None of that mattered. People came into Wrigley Field *knowing* they were comfortable. Just as people who had not been to Comiskey Park in years *knew* it was a crumbling ruin.

"Beautiful Wrigley Field" was a marvelous promotion based on a completely valid premise. The trouble was that I could never get its creator to take the next logical step: to give the customers what they really set out for the ball park hoping to find — entertainment and excitement.

There was only one promotional gimmick I ever got away with. Mr. Wrigley permitted me to install lights on top of the flagpole to let homeward-bound Elevated passengers know whether we had won or lost that day. The flagpole was on top of a new scoreboard, and at its summit I put a crossbar with a green light on one side and a red light on the other. The green light told the El passengers we had won, the red that we had lost.

All right, it wasn't much, but it was all I had and I was proud of it. Not long after it was up, I glanced out the window of my office in the Wrigley Building and saw, to my horror, that a furious wind was whipping down the street. In my mind, I could see my flagpole toppling over. I ran out into the street, grabbed a taxi and headed for the park. (One of the many things Boots and I could never get Mr. Wrigley to do was to move the office to the park so we wouldn't have to spend half our lives traveling back and forth.)

Trees were toppling over all along the route. Windows were being blown out of store fronts. Still, it never occurred to me that I was in the middle of Chicago's worst hurricane in a decade. I had my own problems. I had computed the strains and stresses for the flagpole myself and I was checking over my figures to find out how much of a wind I had allowed for. Arriving at the park, I dashed to the scoreboard and climbed out through the trap door onto the narrow roof.

As soon as I got out there, needless to say, the wind practically blew me back downtown. I grabbed the flagpole and hung on for dear life as it swayed back and forth. The El trains were moving slowly on the tracks behind me, and I could just imagine one homeward-bound fan turning to the guy beside him and saying, "Yeah, I *know* green means we win and red means we lose, but what means a pale-faced young man waving back and forth?"

Eventually, I got Cliff Westcott, who did the real engineering work for us, to check my specifications. He found I had built in 50 percent more stress than would have been needed for the worst hurricane in Chicago history. That wasn't very bright of me. I had wasted Mr. Wrigley's money and I had let down the Lewis Institute. Still, as I thought of myself swaying back and forth on that pole, I cannot say I was too unhappy.

When it came to beautifying Wrigley Field, Mr. Wrigley was open to all suggestions. If he wanted something, money was no object. Time was something else again. Time *was* an object. What Phil Wrigley wants he wants right now.

In planning the construction of the new bleachers, he decided that an outdoor, woodsy motif was definitely called for. Since I had always admired the ivy-covered bleacher walls at Perry Stadium in Indianapolis I suggested that we appropriate the idea for ourselves. Almost absently, I added, "And we can put trees or something in the back."

What I had in mind was a circle of small trees outside the park. Mr. Wrigley didn't want the trees *outside* the park and he didn't want to wait any ten years while they grew up over the bleachers. He wanted them *in* the bleachers, on the steps leading up to the scoreboard, and he wanted them planted full-grown.

What he got were the most expensive tree plantings in the history of the world. Just for openers, we had to build tree boxes into every step, which meant new concrete footings and new steel supporters to carry the weight.

That's a routine construction job, though. From there on in, the routine stopped. Chicago, you see, is situated on Lake Michigan. A strong wind comes off the lake. Someday, a poet is going to give Chicago some kind of appropriate nickname, like, say, The Windy City. We planted all of Mr. Wrigley's giant trees, and a week after we finished, the bleachers looked like the Russian steppes during a hard cold winter. Nothing but cement and bark. The leaves had all blown away.

Mr. Wrigley put that down as bad luck. We pulled out all those barren trees and planted a whole new set of leaf-bearing trees. Along came the wind to blow all those leaves away too. We kept putting in trees, and we kept having bad luck. We could have turned the Grand Canyon into a forest with all the trees we planted, since it took about ten sets of trees before Mr. Wrigley began to spot a trend. The trees were quite inexpensive; the footings cost about $200,000.

That left me with the ivy. I had planned on planting it at the end of the season, after the bleachers had been completely rebuilt. By the time the new season came around, the ivy would have caught and Mr. Wrigley would have his outdoor atmosphere.

The Cubs were ending the season with a long road trip, returning home only in the final week for one last series. The day before the team was to return, Mr. Wrigley called me in to tell me he had invited some people to the park to watch the game and gaze upon his ivy.

"Holy smokes," I said, "I haven't even ordered it yet, let alone planted it. But I'll see what I can do."

John Seys, the vice-president, called a friend who owned a nursery. He informed us that ivy couldn't be put in overnight.

"Well," I said, "what can I put in that will take the place of ivy?"

"Bittersweet," he said.

Bob Dorr, the grounds keeper, and I strung light bulbs all along the fence to enable us to work through the night. When the morning sun broke over the grandstand roof, it shone upon a bleacher wall entirely covered with bittersweet. We had planted the ivy in between, and, in time, the ivy took over.

I spent a sleepless night getting the scoreboard up, too, although I can hardly blame Mr. Wrigley for that one. While I was fooling around with the blueprints, an inventor walked into my office with a working model based upon an entirely new concept. Instead of having lights switching on and off, like all other scoreboards, his model featured brightly painted eyelids which were pulled up and down magnetically.

The inventor was a shy, hesitant, somewhat apologetic man, proof enough for me — out of my long experience scouting inventors — that he was the real thing. In addition, the model worked to perfection. Predictably, Mr. Wrigley was fascinated by it. "This is what we want," he said. "Something different. Just so long as he can have it ready before the end of the season."

I asked my genius if he could have it ready.

You bet your sweet life he could.

The day before the delivery date stipulated on the contract, I phoned his factory to find out what kind of help he was going to need from our ground crew. Nobody answered. I sped immediately to the factory address and found a small second-floor loft. It was deserted.

My genius, I later learned, had invented a great deal in his life but he had never actually built anything this big. Thus, he had assembled all the necessary materials in his loft, had completed a good part of the work, and then, with the moment of truth staring him in the face, he had panicked and run out.

I summoned the ground crew from the park. The wiring, I could see, was similar to switchboard wiring, so I called a friend at Kellogg Switchboard Co. and borrowed a couple of dozen of his electricians. We all rolled up our sleeves and went to work. I drilled the frames. The ground crew put the frames together and the Kellogg electricians wired them. We built the whole scoreboard in that loft during the night, carting it to the park unit by unit, where the park electricians assembled it.

It worked perfectly. It is the scoreboard still being used at Wrigley Field.

Not to leave the story hanging, I paid the inventor every cent the contract called for, without even deducting the amount we had paid the extra help. There was no denying it, his scoreboard did work. Thus heartened and encouraged, he went into the scoreboard business. Every now and then he would write me a chatty letter letting me know how he was getting on. I'd write back telling him about the ball club. Neither of us ever wrote one word about the way he had ducked out on us.

Two years ago, while I was looking around Chicago, without success, for someone to build me an exploding scoreboard for Comiskey Park, my friend phoned me to let me know he wanted to bid on it. By that time, understand, he had a thriving business. "Nothing doing," I said, growing a little indignant twenty years after the fact. "I don't want to have to go out and put this one up myself, too."

There was one thing I was unable to persuade Mr. Wrigley to do, even for the park. In 1934, the year before Larry MacPhail installed the first lights in a major-league stadium, I tried to get Mr. Wrigley to put lights in Wrigley Field. "Just a fad," he said. "A passing fancy."

Every year, I'd bring it up again. Every year he would come up with a new reason for not doing it.

"Those light towers look terrible sticking up there," he'd say. "They'll spoil all this beauty we've worked so hard to create."

I got together with Cliff Westcott and a hydraulic engineering firm to work out a system for placing the "baskets" — the platforms on which lights are mounted — on telescoping towers. During the day, the baskets would be tucked completely out of sight. At night, when they were needed, they would rise out, fully lighted.

That was all well and good, said Wrigley, except that the lights themselves were so garish that they would spoil the effect he had been trying to create for his beautiful field.

OK. I got Westinghouse to run tests on lighting a field with fluorescents. They found it could be done. Mr. Wrigley, of course, had a reason for not wanting it done that way either. No matter what I came up with, he had a reason for not doing it.

Old men, playing dominoes across the hearth, like to say that Phil Wrigley is the last true baseball man because he is the only owner who still holds, in the simple faith of his ancestors, that baseball was meant to be played under God's own sunlight.

I know better. Having blown the chance to be first with lights, Mr. Wrigley just wasn't going to do it at all.

I could at least talk to him about things like lights. When it came to promotion ideas, he wouldn't even listen. He could tell from some manic gleam in my eye what was coming, and as soon as I opened my mouth, he would say, "No, no, no."

And yet, everybody fools you. Just when you're sure you have somebody figured out down to the soles of his feet, he'll do something to confound you.

One afternoon, I was called to Mr. Wrigley's office. It's a big office with a big desk in front of a big window. Seated in one of the easy chairs alongside the desk was a ferret-faced, wizened little guy in a checkered suit. He was puffing on a cigar in that self-pleased, self-important way that only a cigar can bring out.

You could see that Mr. Wrigley was pleased with himself, too. "He's going to help us," he told me. "He's going to give us a psychological advantage."

From the look of this little bum, I'm thinking that the only psychological advantage he could give us would be to sneak into the visitors' locker room before every game and steal the spikes off their shoes — an assignment for which he seemed eminently suited.

Almost as if he had read my mind, he jumped out of the chair, fixed me with an awesome and terrible glare and began to circle around me, making cobralike passes at me with one hand like Bela Lugosi.

While I was watching this dance, fascinated beyond belief, Mr. Wrigley was comparing his discovery to a wrestling manager who was supposed to be able to put a whammy on his boy's opponents, a wonderful publicity gag that was getting a big play in the Chicago papers.

Holy smokes, I thought, suddenly getting it. Old Phil has come up with a real good one. Who'd have thought the old boy had it in him? I had finally got to him, I figured. Things were going to get interesting around Wrigley Field.

Two days later, during a meeting in Wrigley's office, I began to talk up our whammy man, because I thought it was pretty funny. "What are we holding back for?" I said. "Let me give it to the papers today."

A chill came over the room. "There's nothing funny about this," Mr. Wrigley said evenly. "This man may help us. And don't go talking to your newspaper friends about it. Or anybody else, either."

What can you say to a multimillionaire? I could think of a lot of things. Like, "When I was a boy, my daddy told me that if a little man ever came up to me in a checkered suit, took the cigar out of his mouth and told me he was going to win a pennant for me by putting a whammy on my opponents, I should, despite my sweet and trusting nature, take the elementary precaution of checking him out with the Better Business Bureau for past performance."

He had contracted to pay this guy — may Ford Frick be elected to another term as Commissioner if this is not the truth — a flat $5,000 fee plus an additional $25,000 if we won the pennant.

For the rest of the year we carried our Evil Eye around the league with us. At home, he sat directly behind the plate, gesturing furiously at opposing pitchers, none of whom seemed disposed to enter into the spirit of the thing at all. (He was, I must admit, able to cast his strange spell over the customers sitting nearby, most of whom could be seen edging cagily away from him — which proves that Beautiful Wrigley Field did attract a most discriminating clientele.)

Our man operated under a severe handicap for such a chancy profession. He could not stand cold weather. (Which led me to believe that he was a fraud — not an Evil Eye at all but a voodoo chief who had served his apprenticeship in equatorial Africa.) On cold days, he would go up to the office, stand over the Western Union ticker and put the whammy on the tape as the play-by-play came in.

Let me make it clear that I don't want this to be taken as a blanket indictment of all Evil Eyes. Most Evil Eyes, I'm sure, are honest, tax-paying, respectable citizens. It's only that rotten 3 percent who don't give you an honest day's work for an honest day's pay who give the whole profession a bad name.

David S. Broder

College Haunts,
40 Years After

Washington Post, June 10, 1987

As an antidote to Washington, a weekend in Chicago proves wonderfully instructive in the delights of simplicity. The occasion is a reunion of the class of 1947 at the College of the University of Chicago, an odd lot of adolescents and returning veterans, all of whom had struggled with the mysteries of Plato's Dialogues and the other classics our resident demi-god, Robert Maynard Hutchins, decreed to constitute the heart of a liberal education.

After dinner, our classmate, archeologist Robert McCormick Adams, now the secretary of the Smithsonian Institution, tells us we should not try retroactively to invent a homogeneous culture that had not existed in our student days. But we find in conversation that we had more of a bond than we knew. Almost all of us can summon up with ease the terror we had felt in confronting those formidable works of philosophy, science and literature we had been asked to read and analyze. And all of us can recall the occasional exaltation at discovering, in classroom discussion or dormitory bull session, some glimpse of their meaning.

After the reunion events, I leave the South Side for the North, seeking more wisdom from the contemplation of the past. At least 10 years before I set foot on the Midway — at least 50 years ago, that is — I started going to ball games at Wrigley Field. And Saturday afternoon I confirm what seems increasingly important — that it has not changed at all.

I had last checked it out in 1984. I had loved watching the first two playoff games against the Padres, surrounded by other longtime and long-suffering fans, all of us insulated from foreknowledge that the Cubs were about to blow their pennant chances again. But there was no link to the past in a Cubs–Padres rivalry, no precedent for the Cubs being in a league championship series. It felt very strange watching baseball in October in Wrigley Field.

This Saturday afternoon, by contrast, as the Cubs prepare to play the Cardinals, everything reverberates with tradition. These teams have played each other forever.

Much — perhaps too much — has been written about Wrigley Field's fidelity to baseball's past: the grass surface, the ivy on the outfield walls, the refusal to install lights or play night games. Less noted, but equally important, is the simple fact that Wrigley Field allows baseball, the neighborhood game in every American community, to be played in a neighborhood setting.

Almost every other ballpark, old and new, is surrounded by acres of parking lots; many have spaghetti strands of superhighway circling their perimeters. A few years ago, I tried to walk to a night game at Shea Stadium from the LaGuardia Airport motel where I was staying. The distance was modest, but no sidewalks or surface streets lead to the Mets' home. By the time I had dodged traffic to cross three freeways, I was almost too shook-up to enjoy the game.

Wrigley Field, by contrast, is reached on foot. You walk down city sidewalks, past apartment buildings that look no better or worse than they did 50 years ago. The neighborhood is not being gentrified, and it is not slipping slumward. It is the same as it always has been, and so is the experience inside the park.

You walk in, buy your scorecard, and find your seat — in my case, in a box just beyond first base. The seats are still uncushioned wood; the scoreboard is primitive; and the game is unfolding just a few feet away. Time has stopped. The Cardinal bullpen pitchers, soaking up the sun on a bench just beyond the red brick wall where I have rested my beer, are as fresh-faced (and, in this case, as uniformly white) as were the players I first saw 50 years ago.

It is not until I get back in my rental car, savoring the memories of a satisfying 6–5 win, that the meaning of the reunion and the ball game become clear. I tune in Garrison Keillor's next-to-last "Prairie Home Companion" broadcast and find him answering questions from people in the audience. A man, obviously unhappy at the program's imminent demise, asks plaintively "if we'll ever get another glimpse of Lake Wobegon."

Keillor responds that each of us should be able to construct a far more complete picture of his imaginary village in our minds when he stops giving us the weekly news from Lake Wobegon. He says that he has learned that the fewer details he supplies in his stories, the more convincing the pictures listeners draw for themselves. "I found that if I just didn't get in the way of people's imaginations, they would give me all kind of credit as a storyteller."

That comment is more than charming modesty. It explains why Wrigley Field and the College of the University of Chicago exert such a hold on those who attend them. The ballpark has no electronic scoreboards or other distractions to get in the way of the spectator's experience of the game of baseball. And the Hutchins college, today as then, encourages a direct experience — at whatever level of understanding one can achieve — of the writings of the finest minds of Western civilization.

Keillor is bowing out, but Wrigley Field and the College of the University of Chicago go on, essentially unchanged. And that is something to celebrate in this overgimmicked, overcomplicated world.

Joe Mantegna

Let There Be Light! The Better to See Our Memories

New York Times, August 7, 1988

"And on the seventh day the Lord rested, and came to beautiful Wrigley Field, to watch the Chicago Cubs, play His own game, on His own green grass, under His own lights."

This is the first line uttered by a character I created in the play "Bleacher Bums," more than 10 years ago. To a true Cub fan, all the tangible symbols of devotion — the ivy-covered wall, Brickhouse's "Hey, Hey!" Ernie Banks, Harry Caray's rendition of "Take Me Out to the Ballgame," and all the rest — were always joined by that one intangible: the lack of lights. Well, scratch the intangible.

I haven't, as yet, had the pleasure-displeasure of seeing what Wrigley with lights looks like. They say they've been designed to go with the decor of the park. Maybe they'll let the ivy grow up the framework and curl delicately round each zillion kilowatt bulb. Probably not. I do know it has been a long, tough battle.

On frequent trips back to Chicago I'd see the yellow signs in the windows of the homes round the ball park declaring, "No Lights in Wrigley." I understood their concern. Wrigley Field was the friendly giant. This colossus would swallow up thousands of people on balmy afternoons, and it seemed you could hear the reverberating roar from miles away. The streets round the park would teem with kids with mitts hoping to grab an out-of-the park homer, and neighboring rooftops would fill up with lawn chairs for a true bird's-eye view of that day's event.

But come sundown a strange thing happened. Sunset was the time for all good people to go home to their families and loved ones, and as the neighborhood shops shuttered up for the evening, so did Wrigley. Other teams had rainouts. Only the Cubs had darkouts. The Cub philosophy was simple; baseball was a game of grass and sunlight. Friendly giants sleep at night, but come morning you could be sure that the darkened hulk that loomed over you in Chicago's near-north side would awaken once again to welcome the multitudes coming to pay homage.

They say P. K. Wrigley dropped a little of his gum money during the off season of 1941 and actually bought lights. In December of that year, however, Pearl Harbor created new priorities and P.K. quietly donated the lights to the war effort. He probably also felt he could take a hint.

Day games did create unique problems, though. If you wanted to see a Cub game early in the season or after Labor Day, and it happened to be a weekday, *and* you happened to be a student, there was only one way to do it. A lot of forged "Johnny was sick today" letters made their way to Chicagoland teachers during the ball season. At most parks fans screamed and waved when the TV cameras panned them. Only at Wrigley would you see school kids and businessmen alike ducking from the camera's view so as not to be discovered on the late-night sports report by eagle-eyed principals and bosses.

Friday was Ladies' Day. Once you reached puberty, Friday at Wrigley was paradise. Hordes of halter-tops and bikinis, coming more to tan and wave at cute outfielders than get involved in a ballgame, but if you were a teen-aged boy, who cared! I suppose it will never be quite like that again.

So now, after all the hoopla, after all the passionate feelings on both sides of the lights in the Wrigley Field controversy, what does it all mean? In the sober light of day (sunlight that is), I guess I'm left with the unoriginal feeling that, ultimately, the inevitable does happen.

In the fantasy minds of baseball fans, we love to think of our memories of men and deeds of the diamond as the stuff epic poems are made of. The reality is often something else. I remember when I first went to the Cubs' locker room as a young man of 30, there to do research on the play. At last, face-to-face, I'd meet my heroes! Gods who walked the earth. Prodigious behemoths of countless battles on countless ballfields, who would throw their massive arms round my shoulders and say, "Son, welcome to major league baseball."

What actually happened was I met a roomful of guys mostly younger than I was, with more in common with college kids than the grizzled veterans I imagined. The final blow; they called me *Mr.* Mantegna! *My* Cubs, the mythical men on the baseball cards had frozen in time in my mind only. Roger Kahn was right. They are the boys of summer. And when the boys become men too old to play a boys' game, new boys take their place.

So what does this all have to do with lights at Wrigley? Just this. I'll remember the Wrigley of the sunlight. Fondly. Just like my dad remembered the Wrigley Field with the wooden fences, or my grandfather remembered the one with *no* fences. Maybe that's why we have change. So we have something to lock away in a secret part of our memory to be divulged at a later date to our children and grandchildren. From this day on, no baby born will know Wrigley totally without lights. But for that matter, no baby born will ever gaze at a moon that's been unwalked by man. Times change. Things change. Some for the better, some not. An era is over, a page has been turned.

Will lights in Wrigley have much impact on the world in general? Of course not. Will it even help the Cubs become a more competitive team? Probably not. But one thing will happen. I, and countless others, will sit in the bleachers some summer night with our own pint-sized fans, and amidst their protests we'll bore them with the statement, "I remember when . . .".

I started this with jumbled Genesis; I'll end with it. "Let there be light!" What kind of light is not what's important. What's important is, "Let there be baseball!"

Bernie Lincicome

The Sun to Set on Cubs' Illusions

Chicago Tribune, August 8, 1988

On this date in history, or near enough, the only American president to ever leave office in disgrace gave up the world.

And Wrigley Field gave up its innocence.

Only a fool, or a Mets fan, would confuse which one contains the greater shame.

I will take a pass on the lighting of Wrigley Field. It is an easy choice. Whenever possible I avoid the soiling of virgins.

The great, jangling street hustle that has preceded the event is worth neither the noise nor the souvenirs.

The loss of innocence is too precious to end up on a T-shirt. You do not strike commemorative coins for an execution. Maybe you do. This is my first.

This is not about night baseball, not about the Cubs, not about which way the wind blows after dark. Not about electricity.

This is not about property values or cable wars or corporate greed or common sense.

This is about dread and regret and the death of illusions. This is about fearing the world will be less tomorrow than it is today.

This is about wishes and memories and generations holding hands.

And all the logic and all the candlepower in the world will not illuminate it as something else.

The Cubs do not play baseball in a stadium. They play in a metaphor. Wrigley Field passed from being just a ballpark when, I'm only guessing, oh, when Pete LaCock was playing first base.

Or was that Peter Pan?

Wrigley Field is as ephemeral as Camelot, and as necessary.

It is the antidote to future shock, a reminder that the world got along perfectly fine without microwaves and spray paint and coffee whitener.

It is a shining sanctuary from the possible. And its occupants are living reminders that not only isn't winning the only thing, it isn't even necessary.

So rarely has the destiny of a sports franchise been as clear as that of the Cubs.

The Cubs are baseball's poster children, winsome and blameless. They never need to be forgiven for being as they are, for they cannot help it.

The Cubs are absolutely free of all expectations, unburdened by past excellence, immune from the urgency to prove they deserve to be adored.

The Cubs are as privileged as royalty, having done nothing to earn affection other than allowing it.

The Cubs have won a World Series. There are still a few witnesses alive to testify to it. The Cubs have won a pennant since the beginning of the nuclear age, if only by a few months. They have been models of restraint.

The Cubs are heartbreak-proof, no more capable of inflicting pain than statues in a park, one of their frequent disguises.

All of this is made tolerable only in the fairyland of ivy and bare skin, in the Cubs' own special world of Daylight Fantasy Time.

Night baseball at Wrigley Field eliminates one more lie, and we need lies. We need to believe in what is unreal, for truth kills imagination.

The truth is, you turn on lights to work. Recess never needed electricity.

The Cubs, our proxies, have lost the excuse of perpetual childhood, an amnesty possible only in natural, dependable daylight.

It is time to grow up.

Sunshine makes shadows; night makes secrets.

George F. Will

Take Me Out to a Night Game

Newsweek, August 15, 1988

What is wrong with this picture? Nothing. But bitter controversy swirls around the things that cast the shadow on the grass in the picture. The picture is of Wrigley Field, where the Chicago Cubs have played daytime baseball since 1916. The shadow is cast by light standards. There will be night games at Wrigley. "The horror, the horror," say shocked "tourists." But their position is pure malarkey.

Playing some night games will enhance something that can stand a bushel and a peck of enhancing — the Cubs' competitiveness. The Cubs will play fewer games in the sauna of Midwestern summer afternoons. They will have less difficulty adjusting to the sharp difference between their home and away schedules.

Real baseball purists want to see the game played well. That consideration seems decidedly secondary to many Cub fans who natter on and on and on about the Wrigley Field ambience, gestalt, "experience," etc. While they are waxing poetic and semitheological about the sunshine (which can be found elsewhere) and the democracy of the bleachers (a democracy of, by and for the people privileged enough to skip work in the afternoon), the Cubs are getting waxed by better teams. Too many Cub fans seem to think that, leaving aside the mundane business of batting and pitching and fielding, the Cubs are, morally, a cut above the other 25 major-league teams. Such fans think of the Cubs as baseball's Williamsburg, a cute, quaint artifact of historic preservation. They say lights are horrid because the Cubs are custodians of sacred tradition.

In 1913, when Churchill was a young First Lord of the Admiralty, some stuffy men accused him of traducing the traditions of the British Navy. "And what are they?" replied Churchill. "They are rum, sodomy and the lash." Wrigley Field's most conspicuous tradition is mediocre baseball. The Cubs have not won a pennant since 1945, the year the Dow Jones high was 195, *Carousel* opened on Broadway and a hit song was "On the Atchison, Topeka and Santa Fe." The song was about passenger trains. The Cubs have not won a World Series since 1908, two years before Mark Twain died. The Cubs are now in the 80th year of their rebuilding effort. If — when — they fail to win the pennant this year they will break a record previously held by the St. Louis Browns: the longest span (43 years) without winning a league championship. In the seasons 1946 through 1987 the Cubs won 3,033 games and lost 3,567, putting them 534 games below .500 for that period. As this is written, they are below .500 this season. They could go undefeated in the 1989, 1990 and 1991 season and still be below .500 for the postwar era. Real Cub fans should say of tradition, "Enough already."

I will wager dollars against doughnuts that 99 $^{44}/_{100}$ths percent of all the "baseball purists" who have worked themselves into a tizzy about Wrigley's lights are not even serious fans. They are dime-store esthetes cultivating a pose of curmudgeonliness, confusing that with a delicate sensibility. As they rhapsodize about Wrigley Field, untroubled by the esthetic shortcomings of the baseball played there, they sound like those fishermen who say it is not catching fish that matters, it is the lapping of the water against the boat and the murmuring of the breeze in the pines — the ambience, gestalt, experience, etc. Fiddlesticks. People satisfied with fishless fishing will not catch fish and are not real fishermen. People satisfied with the Wrigley Field experience — see them swoon about the ivy on the outfield walls — should be as serious about baseball as they are about botany.

When next you see a Cub fan theatrically suffering the vapors at the mere mention of being deprived of day baseball 18 times a year (that is the night-game limit until the year 2002) ask them to answer under oath this question: how often do you actually go to Wrigley Field to savor the ambience, gestalt, experience, etc.? Remember, baseball fans, like fishermen, fib. For example, you cannot swing a cat by the tail anywhere in America without conking on the head someone who swears that he or she spent his or her formative years in Brooklyn's Ebbets Field and that the cup of joy was forever dashed from his or her lips when the Dodgers went West. But if all the sentimentalists who say these things had really passed through the Ebbets Field turnstiles a tenth as often as they say, the Dodgers would still be in Brooklyn.

There have been night games in major-league baseball since 1935. Fifty-three years constitutes a considerable tradition in an institution only 112 years old (the National League, "the senior circuit," was founded in 1876). And were it not for Pearl Harbor, the Cubs today would be in their fifth decade of night baseball. Material for light standards had been bought and was donated to the war effort.

There is today too much estheticization of judgments. Dukakis is "Zorba the clerk." Bush is preppie. But peace and prosperity are at stake. The point of politics is good government, not the display of charm. And the point of a baseball team is good baseball, not inferior play somehow redeemed by a pretty setting. Part of the Cubs' problem may be that too many Cub fans have an attitude problem. They are too devoted to the wrong thing. Let there be lights.

Tom Callahan

Aweary of the Sun

Time, August 22, 1988

Trains are still the best conveyance for transporting a mood. Last week's destination was either the past or the future — Chicago anyway. Wrigley Field. After two or three switchyards, a traveler gets turned around, and the sensation is of highballing one way and the other, backward and forward, in time.

The pity with which the old fedora-wearing baseball writers beheld their fresh replacements always seemed to have to do with missing trains. Seeing the country roll by in thatches of shadows, hearing Babe Ruth call all the redcaps "Stinkweed," were trivial elements of the coverage but critical parts of the experience. Without day baseball and night Pullmans, Red Smith could never have written, "Frisch's homer was the longest in history. Frankie talked about it all the way from St. Louis to Boston."

But railroad tracks don't sing anymore. Sinatra barely sings anymore. The new sleeping compartments are capsules resembling John Glenn's old accommodations on exhibit in the Air and Space Museum (without the air and space). And all the ball clubs have long since flown away. Wrigley Field fell in line with the age last week, when, 53 years after the innovator (Cincinnati) and 40 years since the procrastinator (Detroit), the Cubs finally put in lights. That makes everyone.

The Governor isn't often present for the throwing of the

switch, but this was an unusual sunset. Even the buildings
across the street wore bunting. A World Series supply of
chroniclers from the American as well as the National League
showed up to see the last-place Phillies oppose the fourth-
place Cubs, whose proprietors said they had to give in to
television and go incandescent or risk having to host every
one of their postseason games in St. Louis. If any. The Cubs
are 80 years between World Championships and pennantless
since World War II.

Their longest-suffering fan, a hearty, hatchet-faced former
tire dealer named Harry Grossman, 91, pushed the electric
button. "Let there be light," he proclaimed in a biblical voice.
The Cubs' holiest relics, Ernie Banks and Billy Williams,
threw out first balls. Chicago's most sentimental pitcher, Rick
Sutcliffe, took the mound. "It's like sunshine and Wrigley are
saying goodbye to each other," he thought, though only eight
night games are scheduled this season and just 18 a year for
the calculable future. Looking hard at the Phillies' leadoff
man, Phil Bradley, and straight into a light show of Instamatic
flashes, Sutcliffe was struck by history — and Bradley.

A home run right off the bat, the perfect note played on a
party horn. Then the bottom of the inning kept on that way,
fast and farfetched. Mitch Webster singled and Ryne Sandberg was up. Out of the rightfield stands popped Morganna,
the floppy exhibitionist with the unmissable kisser, racing for
the batter's box on mincing old-ballplayer feet that brought
back the newsreels. She couldn't make it past the security
guards to Sandberg, but she got to him anyway. His giggling
homer gave Chicago a 2–1 lead.

Later, an inning short of the official seal, poetry struck a
final time, along with lightning. Funnels of dust that some
took to be divine displeasure rose up and blew across the
infield, and two hours of rain flooded the tarpaulin and washed
out the game. The sellout crowd of 39,008 drew back under
cover and took the time to really look at the old place in the
new light. The outfield wall, with its singular vines and
morning glories and spider webs, was humanely spared any

hardware. The stanchions peek fairly unobtrusively over the shoulders of the stadium. The park, that is. Or that was.

To lighten the mood, by ones and threes the spryest fans took slides on the tarp, ultimately including a pretty girl in a pink dress. Making a case for lenient court fines, four Cubs took flying dives on their own stomachs, including the pitcher Les Lancaster, who happens to be on the disabled list after an appendectomy. It's actually a promising young team, and if Chicago does play better over the next couple of summers, people will say it was the cooler August nights, and maybe they will be right.

It makes no sense and does no good to lament little deteriorations on every side. Constant comparisons with better old days are illusory and unreliable. It's enough to say we used to have Spencer Tracy and Katharine Hepburn and now we have Michael Douglas and Cher. If anything has been lessened at Wrigley Field, it is probably something quite small, certainly nothing to cry over, only a momentary feeling of letdown, like missing the train.

DRAMATIS PERSONAE

They say baseball is the "thinking man's sport," aspiring to the sublime by virtue of RBI's, ERA's, LOB's and other statistical esoterica. Still, it's hard to imagine how anybody could care less were it not for the full spectrum of color brought to the game via the personalities of its practitioners. And the Cubs, if not statistically competitive with most other teams in recent times, can certainly hold their own when it comes to piquant personages. Of course, we've heard all kinds of stories about the likes of Cap Anson, King Kelly, Charlie Grimm, Gabby Hartnett, and all the other colorful Cub greats of bygone days. But there's also plenty of entertainment and enlightenment to be gleaned from the lesser-heralded Cubs of yesteryear, as well as some of the more recent Cub stars, as the following collection of essays will testify.

A couple of specimens of *bruinus anonymous,* Hardrock Johnson and Emil Verban, are given their respective days in the sun by Ira Berkow. Sandwiched between those two Berkow pieces are mini-profiles of Cub stars and non-stars of the '40s, '50s, and '60s, by Brendan C. Boyd and Fred C. Harris, who freely exercise their talent for saving certain careers from the profound and perpetual anonymity they so richly deserve. But lest we dwell too heavily on the obscure, Mark Kram's "Tale of Two Men" promises to give us the lowdown on both Hack Wilson and Ernie Banks, though in the end it's really an extended paean to Mr. Cub. And we cap off our humble tribute to the Warriors of Wrigleyville with a few ponderings on a pair of formidable Williamses: Raymond Coffey's brief and unequivocal testimonial to new Hall-of-Famer Billy, and Mike Downey's lively monograph on fireballer Mitch.

Ira Berkow

Mr. Hardrock, Sir

New York Times, April 5, 1986

Hardrock Johnson died. He was 90 years old.

The short obituary on him in a recent issue of *The Sporting News* sent a sportswriter back in time, to a summer's day in Chicago in 1951, when an 11-year-old boy stood under the stands at Wrigley Field after a game and, along with his pals and numerous other fans, sought autographs from the Cubs who emerged from the clubhouse, looking large in slicked-down hair and wide sport jackets.

A Cub coach named Roy (Hardrock) Johnson hurried through the crowd to the nearby parking lot. He was a leathery man, gruff-looking but with a pigeon-toed walk that seemed to suggest a vulnerability below the tough exterior.

The boy followed and importuned him for his autograph. Johnson said he was in a hurry, couldn't sign. As he slammed his car door, about a millimeter or so from the boy's pencil and the boy's fingers, Johnson said, "Come to the park tomorrow, kid, and I'll give you a baseball."

Silly boy, said the 11-year-old's associates, Hardrock ain't givin' you no ball.

"He said he would," said the true believer.

The next day — or so it seems in memory, though it may have been two days later, or a week — the boy and his pals returned to the ball park. It was well before the start of the game, and the Cubs in their white uniforms were practicing on that stunningly clean green and brown field.

And there, along the first-base line, hitting fungoes to the outfielders, was Hardrock Johnson, No. 42.

The kid remembers the flight down the concrete stairs from the grandstands to the short barrier that divided the box seats from the playing field. He remembers the smell of the hot dogs sizzling on the vendors' grills, the scratchy recording on the public-address system ("Goodnight, Sweetheart" always seemed to be playing), and the soggy hole — from the peach his mother had packed — that was forming in the brown lunch bag he carried. And he remembers his lofty expectations.

"Mr. Hardrock, sir," called the boy. "I'm the kid you promised a ball to."

Mr. Hardrock, sir, kept hitting fungoes. High fungoes that hung in the blue sky, and then fell. The boy called to the coach again, and again. Nothing. Some adults sitting nearby tittered. Soon a heavy hand clamped on the boy's shoulder, accompanied by the usher's dulcet tones: "Get outta here."

The boy began the forlorn climb away from the field when he heard, "Hey, kid." It was Hardrock. He tossed him a baseball.

Up the stairs the boy flew. He remembers holding the ball tightly as the other guys looked it over. Then he sat down with it, rubbed his fingers over the red stitching, and inspected the dirt and grass smudges. He'll never forget the smell of that ball. There is a distinct, unforgettable muskiness to the tanned horsehide of a baseball, but this one also held the aroma of the ball field, and the kid loved it.

In the neighborhood, there were suggestions on how to get the ball clean. The most impressive argument was made for immersing the ball in a bowl of milk. This the kid did. A few days later, he removed it. The ball had turned yellow as parchment.

Nonetheless, he took it back and asked Hardrock to sign it. "I gave you the ball to play with," Johnson said, "not to put on a shelf." He signed it, but the boy did eventually play with it. The stitching came apart, and the cover fell off and the ball was a mass of string. Then it disappeared for all time.

Through the years the incident of getting that baseball from Hardrock Johnson stayed with the boy. It enlarged possibilities for him.

And through the years, as a sportswriter, he would occasionally ask someone with the Cubs what and how Hardrock was doing.

Johnson left the Cubs as a coach in 1954 — he had been struck by a baseball and suffered from a bad hip — and began scouting for the Cubs in the Southwest. Johnson lived in Scottsdale, Ariz., and the sportswriter thought one day he'd visit him and, after all these years, thank him for that baseball. But it never materialized.

Then came the news that Johnson had died, in a nursing home. He had lived there with his wife, Fanetta.

The sportswriter called Mrs. Johnson. She is 86, and her voice sounded clear over the long-distance wires.

"Some people called him 'Hardrock' because he used to work the pitchers so hard," she said, "but most people called him 'Grumpy,' including me and our daughter and even our grandchildren. But living with Roy was wonderful. We just laughed. We had the best time our whole 70 years together. He had that grumpy look, and sometimes his temper was short, but usually it didn't mean anything."

The couple were from Haileyville, Okla. To avoid becoming a coal miner like his father, Roy first became a prize fighter. It wasn't long before he understood that this was as tough a way to earn a living as digging coal, and turned to baseball, and pitching. He was a big leaguer for one season, with Connie Mack's last-place Philadelphia A's of 1918. Johnson won one game and lost five.

He would tell about pitching to Babe Ruth, who was then making his reputation as a slugger with the Red Sox. "Roy said that Mr. Mack told him, 'This guy can hit,'" recalled Mrs. Johnson. "He said, 'Don't give him anything. Make him bite. Or walk him if you have to.' Roy threw and the Babe hit the ball 400 feet into the last row of the bleachers. Roy said,

'It might have cleared the Bunker Hill monument, but at least I didn't walk him.'"

After 1918, Johnson spent many years in the minor leagues, playing, and then managing, in towns like Bisbee, Ariz., and Fort Bayard, N.M., and Ottumwa, Iowa. In 1935 he came up as a coach with the Cubs.

"Roy," said Mrs. Johnson, "loved to work. He was going out and sitting in a beach chair to scout high school and college games until just a year or so ago. And, you know, when he died he still had his teeth."

"Still had his teeth," the sportswriter repeated. "That's nice, that's very nice." And he meant it.

Brendan C. Boyd and Fred C. Harris

From *The Great American Baseball Card Flipping, Trading and Bubble Gum Book*

Bill Nicholson

Bill Nicholson was nicknamed "Swish" somewhat cruelly, and not for the reason you're probably thinking. Swish did one of two things when he came to bat: either he struck out or he hit a home run. There was no middle ground. He led the National League in the early forties in RBI's (twice), and in home runs (also twice). He was always, even in his last years with the Phillies as a pinch-hitter, a long ball threat. It was imperative that he hit home runs as he got older, though, because it was questionable whether he could get around the bases in any kind of hurry with all of the weight he carried then.

Frank Baumann

Frank Baumann was a charter member of the "He Lost It in the Army" club — a curious assortment of mediocre ballplayers that resurrects itself every ten years or so, shortly after the United States has managed to extricate itself once again, more or less successfully, from another round of debilitating foreign entanglements. Membership in the club is open to any

Tightin'
Phillies

BILL NICHOLSON

Bill Nicholson

CUBs

PITCHER
FRANK BAUMANN

ballplayer who has ever belonged to any armed service for any length of time and who now plays lousy. The player in question is entitled by his membership to be excused by press, radio, television, management, and himself for his inept performances with the explanation that, although he was a red hot prospect at the time of his entry into his country's service, somehow the time spent away from the game and the tremendous burden of his military duties have dulled his almost superhuman physical prowess. Members are never established players — who seem curiously immune to the sapping effects of these prolonged layoffs — but always untried youngsters — bonus babies and highly touted rookies —whom owners and general managers have been promoting ruthlessly in an effort to prop up the rapidly diminishing reputations of their sagging franchises. Frank Baumann was a member in good standing of the Korean War chapter of the club — stateside division, one oak-leaf cluster. The story on him was that he had lost the velocity on his fast ball while sitting around some of Mother Army's more decrepit southern encampments on his ample derriere while other less talented and less patriotic youngsters were gaining good seasoning experience in the low minors. (Actually I have always thought that a more cogent explanation for his arm problems might have been that he injured it by lifting a particularly hefty forkful of mashed potatoes up to his bovine craw.)

Jim Brosnan

Jim Brosnan was the rarest of athletic types — the intellectual. Or at least he was what passes for an intellectual in the singularly unenlightened area of professional gamesmanship, which of course is not necessarily the same thing. Brosnan made being intelligent respectable among the jocks and, what's more, he made it pay. He was the first of the resident Boswells of the base paths and also probably the best.

In some of the more basic sports — such as hockey, boxing, horse racing and pocket billiards — an intellectual is anybody who can sign an autograph without his business manag-

er's assistance. In the airier climes of professional football and basketball, however, more stringent standards are needed to measure the relative mental capacities of the combatants. Here style is everything, content nothing, so that only the didactic likes of Frank Ryan, the Cleveland Brown quarter-back/mathematician whom Chris Schenkel delighted in calling Dr. Ryan, are considered worthy of the lofty title "intel-lectual." You know, somebody who specializes in wry, self-effacing postgame interviews and takes a lot of graduate courses in the off-season. But in baseball, the great American leveler, the question of a man's intellectual status is a simple matter of deduction: if a player keeps books in his locker then he's an intellectual. If not, not. It makes no difference that the books are by Harold Robbins or Grace Metalious or that they remain unread throughout the entire length of the season; the simple fact of their existence automatically entitles their owner to be considered something of a sage by the sports-writers and to be nicknamed by his teammates "the profes-sor." This is part of American folklore and nobody's ever going to be able to change it. Well, Jim Brosnan not only read all the books in his locker (and there were some pretty hard books in there too); he even went so far as to write a couple himself. In fact, *The Long Season* and *Pennant Race* were the precursors of the seemingly endless stream of diary-style, eavesdropping chronicles of the sporting life which have been pouring down the literary drainspout for the past decade and a half.

On the back of his card we are informed that "Jim writes short stories in his spare time." Now, if that isn't the hallmark of an honest-to-goodness intellectual, I'll be damned if I know what is.

Harry Lowrey

Harry "Peanuts" Lowrey might have been a grain salesman if he hadn't gone into organized baseball. He played for thirteen years with a number of teams, and is best remembered, if remembered at all, for his pinch hitting. In 1952 and 1953

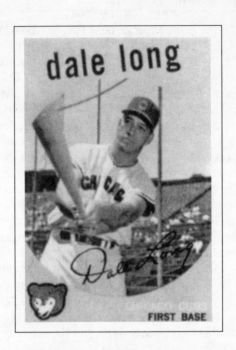

dale long

FIRST BASE

RUSS MEYER

pitcher CHICAGO CUB

Peanuts led the league in pinch hits. The nickname had to do with the fact that most all of those pinch hits were singles, but I'm sure his managers were happy to take them any way they came.

Dale Long

Unlike most players of undistinguished habit, Dale Long was granted two separate and distinct moments of baseball glory. The first came when he hit home runs in eight consecutive ball games for the Pirates in 1956, thus establishing a new major league record. The second came when he was picked up late in his career (1962) by the New York Yankees for their annual late September pennant drive and proceeded to propel them almost singlehandedly into the World Series against the Dodgers. He now hosts a nightly ten-minute sports roundup for an Albany, New York, television station, reading long lists of A.P. box scores, Saratoga High School track team results, and Scolharie County fishing reports in the same flat, colorless style that always characterized his play around the first base bag.

Russ Meyer

Russ Meyer was called "The Mad Monk" for reasons not totally clear to me. He was moderately successful as a pitcher for several National League teams in the fifties, and I remember in particular his very good fast ball for the Phillies during their glory year(s). Russ had a knack for signing on with pennant winners: the Phillies in 1950 and the Brooklyn Dodgers in 1953 and 1955. He also had a knack for getting injured (ankle, shoulder, back) and one felt that he was one of those players who might have been a star if only . . .

Moe Drabowsky

Moe Drabowsky, who grew up collecting baseball cards in Ozanna, Poland, didn't have too many winning seasons as a pitcher for teams in both leagues, but until he joined the Orioles in 1966 (when he finished the season 6–0), he didn't play for many winning teams. Moe was of the Billy Loes

moe drabowsky

CHICAGO CUBS
PITCHER

HARRY CHITI

catcher CHICAGO CUBS

school of players — sleepy-looking — but at 6'3", and with a complicated pitching motion and good stuff, Moe was hard to hit. In what was his greatest single game, in the 1966 World Series, Moe went 6⅔ innings, striking out 11 and getting credit for the win.

Harry Chiti

It is a common prejudice concerning catchers that they are slow — both with their feet and with their wits. Regarding intelligence, naturally I can't answer for many major league catchers, although I once spoke with Lou Berberet in the Red Sox parking lot and I have seen Johnny Bench on any number of television talk shows, and while neither of these gentlemen has impressed me as a rival to Elfrida Von Nardroff in terms of native mental prestidigitation, I don't think you could exactly call them stupid either. But as far as running is concerned . . . now there you really have something. Major league catchers come in three foot-speeds — slow, slower, and slowest. I have no idea why this is, except that they are generally bulky men, with massive thighs and ample derrieres, who spend a great percentage of their waking hours hunched over and squatting at the knees, a position not exactly conducive to increasing the springing power of the legs. The slowest catchers of recent times have been Bob Tillman, a power-hitting catcher-first baseman with the Red Sox in the early sixties whom I once saw almost thrown out at first from the outfield, Earl Battey, who was a good receiver with the Twins and the White Sox for a dozen years and a rival to John Roseboro in the black Buddha look-alike derby, and Harry Chiti, a reserve catcher with any number of teams over a period of any number of years who looked like everybody's brother-in-law, and played like him too. Fortunately for Harry, his lack of speed was not as noticeable as was the others' because he was such a lousy hitter that he rarely got on base. The only time you really noticed how slow he was was when he was trotting back to the dugout after striking out.

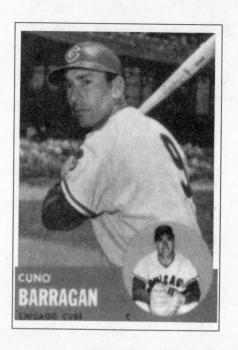

CUNO
BARRAGAN
CHICAGO CUBS

SAM JONES
pitcher CHICAGO CUBS

Cuno Barragan
Who the hell is Cuno Barragan? And why are they saying those terrible things about him?

Sam Jones
Four things and four things only do we know about Samuel Jones.
  (1) That he was born in Stewartsville, Ohio, and lived in Monongah, West Virginia.
  (2) That he never owned a hat that really fit him.
  (3) That he had a toothpick surgically attached to his lower lip.
  (4) And that if anyone ever deserved to be called Sad Sam, it was Sad Sam Jones of Monongah.

Steve Bilko
According to the Peter Principle, the upward mobility of the individual corporate employee in the American free enterprise system is based on his mastering of succeeding levels of competence while progressing on to his ultimate level of

TOBY ATWELL
catcher CHICAGO CUBS

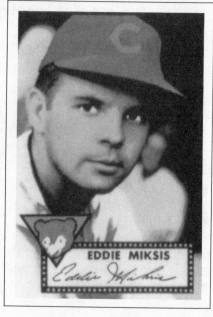

EDDIE MIKSIS

incompetence — that area where the depth and range of his responsibilities are simply too great for the scope of his talents. For Steve Bilko the entire major league infrastructure was that level of incompetence. If Rochester was New York City, Steve Bilko would be in the Hall of Fame.

But it isn't.

And he isn't.

Big Steve tore apart the Piedmont League but he couldn't get arrested in the bigs. The first and last lines on the back of this card tell it all. "Hailed as another Jimmy Foxx in 1945. Had the second highest number of RBIs in the history of the Carolina League. In 1949 hit four homers in one day. Optioned to Rochester in 1952."

I wonder who had the highest number of RBIs in the history of the Carolina League.

Toby Atwell

Toby Atwell has to be remembered by any serious collector of baseball cards in 1952 as having been one of the most difficult cards to acquire. He played for the Cubs that year, as pretty much their regular catcher, and later bounced around the National League as a second-string catcher for another five years before giving it up. But the career of Toby Atwell as player was secondary to the career of Toby Atwell as baseball card, and if you needed him to complete your set too, you'll know what I mean.

Eddie Miksis

The nicest thing that Topps could figure out to say about Eddie Miksis was that he was tenth in the National League in stolen bases in 1951, with 11. Hardly an earthquaking statistic after seven years in the majors. He had a lifetime batting average of .236 and 44 career home runs. Miksis was the sort of guy that if you were introduced to him at a party and he told you he was a big league ballplayer, you'd think he was kidding.

In a way he would have been.

KEN
HUBBS
CHICAGO CUBS

CUBS

ERNIE BANKS 1st base

Ken Hubbs

Just as the fifties was a bad decade for rock and roll singers traveling in private airplanes — Buddy Holly, Richie Valens, the Big Bopper — so was the sixties a bad decade for professional athletes traveling in private airplanes — Rocky Marciano, Tony Lema, Rafael Ossuna.

Kenny Hubbs was an extremely promising young second baseman with the Chicago Cubs, .287 batting average in 1964, rookie of the year at twenty-two. He was killed in the crash of a private plane over Provo, Utah, on February 23, 1965.

We still remember you, Kenny.

Ernie Banks

Ernie Banks, "Mr. Cub," needs no introduction. He was one of those great players who was cursed to play out his career with an inferior team. It is no exaggeration to say that the difference between an Ernie Banks and a Mickey Mantle is the good fortune to play with a championship team. Ernie Banks never had that good fortune. Still, there was something about him that even opponents' fans applauded.

Ira Berkow

Emil the Antelope Returns

New York Times, July 7, 1985

To his left was one great home run hitter, to his right was another great home run hitter, and together the three of them had hit a career total of 1,034 major league home runs. Their lockers, simply by coincidence, had been placed in a row in the National League clubhouse for the recent Cracker Jack Old-Timers' Baseball Classic at R.F.K. Stadium in Washington.

Above the cubicle on his left was the name Willie McCovey, who had hit 521 home runs, and above the cubicle on his right was the name Eddie Mathews, who had hit 512 home runs.

Inscribed above his locker was his name, Emil Verban, who in 1948 hit the only home run of his seven-year major league career as a second baseman for the Cardinals, Phillies, Cubs and Braves.

With his gold-trimmed glasses glittering, and carrying a discernible paunch under his light-blue summer suit, Verban, gray haired at age 69, hurried into the clubhouse, fairly tore away at his clothes and quickly climbed into his baseball suit. He had a pair of baseballs with him and turned to Mathews. Would Eddie autograph the balls? Verban then asked others like McCovey and Aaron and Wilhelm and Banks and Koufax to sign his baseballs.

"Know who that is?" he said to someone nearby, as an elderly, bow-legged man in an American League uniform came in. "That's Luke Appling." Then: "Hi Luke!" said Verban. Appling returned the cordiality, though it wasn't certain whether he knew his greeter's name.

After a while Verban took a seat in an empty cubicle and looked around, seeming almost forlornly out of place among the host of great names.

What was an obscure player like Verban doing here?

Verban, it turns out, is a popular figure in Washington, though he lives in Lincoln, Ill. There is a Washington-based Chicago Cubs fan club and it is named in his honor, the Emil Verban Memorial Society. One of its members is President Reagan, who broadcast Cub games on the radio in the 1930's.

The society was founded 10 years ago, when the Cubs were spending as they often did, a considerable amount of time in the lowest depths of the National League standing.

The name Verban was chosen by club founders as a symbol of the Cubs. To some it was a joke. But to at least one man, it wasn't so funny.

"I didn't think I was a mediocre ball player," said Verban. "And when I first heard about this fan club, I didn't care for the idea.

"You know, I've never seen a guy who put on a uniform who I felt I'd have to take my hat off to. I thought that at my position I could play with the best, except maybe someone like Frisch or Hornsby, who had other things, like more power. But I could make the double play as good as anyone, and I don't think anyone ever covered more ground."

Verban hadn't played in the major leagues since 1950, but his records are as clear to him as if it all happened the other day. He played in two All-Star Games and one World Series, making up one-half of the Cardinals' double-play combination with Marty Marion in the 1944 Series against the St. Louis Browns. "I hit .412 and in one game went 3 for 3," he said. In 1947, he struck out only eight times in 540 times at bat. "Someone told me that's an all-time record for second basemen in a season," he said.

He recalled that he had led the league in putouts and assists

and double plays. He also led two years running in errors —
one of those years, 1949, was his only full one with the
Cubs — but perhaps the error mark was an oversight by
Verban, or he considered it not significant in light of the
ground he could cover.

"And I had a lifetime batting average of .272," he said.
"With an average like that today, I'd be making a ton." His
highest salary was $22,000.

There are about 10 Hall of Famers, excluding pitchers,
who have lower career batting averages than Verban, and
two were seated beside him: McCovey batted .270 and
Mathews .271.

"Nowadays, with this Astroturf and these gloves that are
as big as a bushel basket, I would never have made an error,"
he said, laughing, and pounding his fielder's mitt.

"Look at this." He extended his glove. It looked ancient. It
was black with stubby fingers and cracking leather and no
strings between the fingers and a skimpy webbing. "This is
the glove I used in '44, when I was a rookie, and played in the
Series," he said. "I used other gloves later, but I've always
kept this."

He smiled. "That was in the days when they called me 'the
Antelope,'" he said. "That was my nickname. I got it because
I could move pretty quick. But in those days I was 148 pounds
straight up and down. Now I'm 195 pounds. I've attained my
full growth. I guess now they'd call me the Elephant."

Verban, a real-estate broker in commercial property back
here said: "You know, I came to like the Emil Verban Memorial Society. It gave me more exposure than I ever got as a
player. I get about 10 letters a week from people wanting my
autograph.

"And last year they had a banquet here and I was the
featured guest. They had congressmen and a bunch of
important people. And I was invited to the White House with
my wife, Annetta, and my son, Dr. Emil Verban Jr., and my
daughter Barbara Kivittle. The president was very nice. He
said he was glad to meet my acquaintance. He said that they

had picked the right man for the name of the society, and that it was someone who got the most out of his abilities. It was a thrill."

Verban became a member of the society last year. "They gave me number 7," he said, "my number with the Cubs."

Then the venerable Verban went out to warm up for the game. He played catch with a bat boy. In the five-inning game, he was inserted as a pinch-hitter in the last inning. Batting against Mickey Lolich, Verban hit a ground ball to the third baseman, Eddie Yost.

Verban's old wheels churned, but the throw beat him to the bag. He had given it a good try, as he always had, and pulled a muscle in his leg as well.

Mark Kram

A Tale of Two Men
and One City

Sports Illustrated, September 29, 1969

Unlike termites, immortals have seldom been in residence at
Wrigley Field. The last colossus was one Hack Wilson, an
endomorphic (5'6", 190 pounds) outfielder who finished each
game looking like a chimney sweep. He played hard at night,
too. He was religious in his rounds, preferring Al Capone's
clubs, where he looked like some stumpy Italian cardinal
dispensing to the poor. By morning he could be found
slumbering in a tub full of ice in the clubhouse. His most
famous words were: "Have another beer." He died in a gutter
and is buried in Martinsburg, W. Va. beneath a simple in-
scription:

ONE OF BASEBALL'S IMMORTALS,
LOUIS R. (HACK) WILSON, RESTS HERE.

More than two decades melted in Wrigley's afternoon sun
before the stockbrokers from LaSalle Street, all the saloon
caretakers of the North Side and all the kids who were just
starting their exodus from city blocks to suburbia could
embrace another player of Wilson's stature. His name was
Ernie Banks. The only thing he and Wilson had in common
was the fact that neither ever refused to sign an autograph.

Other than that, Banks was built like a letter opener, comported himself in the manner of a man applying for a loan and relished his work; the only thing he disliked about playing two games was that he could not play three. His most famous words were, and still are, even in these dour last weeks that have not always treated the Cubs kindly: "Welcome to the friendly confines of Wrigley Field. Oh, oh, it's great to be alive and a Cub on this beautiful sun-kissed afternoon."

That was the way he was when he came up in 1953, and he has never changed. After 16 distinguished years baseball's Edgar Guest is a certainty to be marbleized one day at Cooperstown, the place that has tenaciously ignored Hack Wilson. Hack still holds the NL record for home runs, with 56, and the major league RBI record, with 190, but what are you going to do with a guy who, after being admonished for visiting Capone's box at Wrigley, says: "Well, he comes to our place, why shouldn't I go to his?" Clearly, Hack had an image problem, something Ernie Banks will never have — unless Eldridge Cleaver becomes Commissioner of Baseball. Ernie, you see, *is* baseball, meaning he is what The Game thinks people should think baseball is.

Conjure up all the sonnets, all the treacle that propagandists and the sentimental have contributed to the glorification of The Grand Old Game, and that is Ernie. He is — well, mustard on a kid's face, Babe Ruth promising a home run to a boy in the hospital, the smell of spring and an old, cracking boyhood glove, and all those memories and moments and everything that is a symbol of America. Never mind the Hack Wilsons, just give them Kate Smith — or, better yet, Ernie Banks. But unlike many players before him, those with their institutional patter and cellophane politics, Ernie Banks is an original. By just *being,* he is the greatest promoter baseball has ever had. "He's a hundred billboards on a hundred highways," says Frank Lane. "He's priceless as advertising."

It does not matter to Banks that the game he is pushing is hardly the tranquil, sacred chunk of Americana it once was, a game of joy and grateful, uncomplaining serfs, a game of few issues and even fewer answers. The euphoria, of course, is long gone, but one would never know it around Banks. His spirit is indestructible, and you always know baseball is near when Banks, like the geese honking north, almost every year predicts unflinchingly that the Cubs will win the pennant; not even the old 10-team races envisioned by Joe Cronin and Warren Giles in their annual newspaper columns achieved more fame. No wonder, then, that Banks moonlights doing commercials for a cookie called Sunshine. For there are truly no clouds in Ernie's life. When gloom pervades the Cub clubhouse, as it has so often of late, Ernie flashes a sign that reads: "Want to wake up each morning with a smile? Sleep with a hanger in your mouth."

Banks is particularly animated during batting practice, that soft time in baseball when players, like washwomen hanging over a fence, exchange gossip, reveal small injustices to confidants and bolster their egos with prodigious drives into the stands. The area around the cage is Banks' stage, where he performs like some aging vaudevillian. He sings, jabs at some down-home philosophy and jabbers in a weird patois that dwarfs those ordinary apostles of boosterism. If he is in St. Louis he will say: "St. Louis! Home of the mighty Cardinals and the great Stan. St. Louis! Great city. Meet in St. Looie, Looie. . . ." If he is in New York he will say: "New York, the Big Apple, the Melting Pot of the World. Home of *Oh! Calcutta!* and those pesky Mets! East Side, West Side, all around the town. . . ." In Chicago he overflows.

"Henry Aaron," he says, dramatically, looking over at Aaron. "Henry Aaron! The most dangerous hitter who ever lived. Hall of Fame, here he comes. Henry, let's play two today." Aaron, shaking his head, looks at him curiously.

"Oh," continues Banks, "it's great to be alive in beautiful Wrigley Field." Stepping off the paces, he then acts out a gun duel while humming *The Streets of Laredo*. After spinning around and firing, he stops and says, "If everybody loved baseball, if all the kids played it, there would be no shooting in the world."

"Hey, what about Mayor Daley?" he is asked.

"Mayor Daley!" he says. "Mayor Daley! Chicago! My kind of town! Chicago, that toddlin' town. . . ."

Banks also uses the telephone to spread his word. Earlier in the year he called up Frank Robinson in Baltimore and warned that he would be seeing him in October. He called up Lou Brock to say that, as gallant and great as the Cardinals are, it would be sensible for Lou to forget about "a run for our pennant." Once he reached Willie Mays, and this exchange followed:

Banks: Hello. Willie? That you?

Mays (sleepily): Who is this?

Banks: Who is this? It's Ernie Banks. Listen, Willie. First of all, I want to congratulate you on an outstanding performance last night. You're a wonderful player and fine person. You know that, don't you? We won again this afternoon. Did you know that?

Mays: I know that. Don't you think I know what's going on?

Banks: Wonderful. Then you know the Cubs are going all the way. Nothing's going to stop this team.

Mays: Are you calling me to tell me that?

Banks: I'm calling you to tell you to go out there tonight and give it your all against the Cardinals. You're a superstar! I want to see you play like a superstar.

Mays: Who's pitching for them?

Banks (positively, as though this were an advantage): Bob Gibson! You hit him. You always hit him. When you come up to the plate against Gibson it's murder. I feel sorry for him tonight.

Mays (giggling): All right. I got to get dressed to go to the ball park.

Banks: Good. That's positive thinking. And when you get there, remember, you're Willie Mays. No. 24! An immortal!

It is doubtful that Banks has ever thought that he, too, might one day be among the sanctified. The figures, though, those drab, tormenting, frequently mendacious little monsters that terrorize players, guarantee him permanent recognition. True, being with a second-division club practically all of his career, Banks may have faced more than just a humane share of second-line pitching, but that hardly pales the fact that he has been one of baseball's few consistently preeminent hitters. Currently he ranks ninth in alltime home runs, and it is quite possible he could rise as high as sixth before he is through: between 1955 and 1960 he hit more homers — 248 — than anybody in the majors. He has been named the league's Most Valuable Player twice.

Although size does not have much to do with hitting, it is still difficult to imagine Banks having power. His build makes one think of modern sculpture, say a figure made of coat hangers. Where does the power come from? "Ernie," says Clyde McCullough, formerly with the Cubs, "swings a bat like Joe Louis used to throw a punch — short and sweet." Bob Scheffing, one of his many managers, says, "He's got a helluva pair of forearms and wrists. You grab hold of him and it's like grabbing a piece of steel." Once, some years ago, during batting practice Banks' power was the subject of a more or less informal seminar:

"It's his eyes," said Jim Bolger. "Definitely, he's all eyes."

"Maybe," said Walt Moryn. "But I'll take his timing and coordination."

"You're all wrong," concluded Dale Long. "Give me his wrists, and I'll spot each of you 10 home runs before the season starts."

Nearby, grumbling could be heard. Rogers Hornsby, then a Cub batting coach, was talking to himself. He walked over to the theorists and said: "Good eyes, timing, wrists and follow-through." He turned away, leaving behind a loud silence. Rogers had spoken, and his words were like those carved on tablets.

Yet there are a few other aspects that help explain Banks' ability. For one thing, early in his career he began using a 31-ounce bat that, along with his wrists, provided him with flashing bat speed; he could wait till the last microsecond and flick at a ball that was only six inches from the catcher's glove. (He is now back to 35 ounces in an effort to cut down on his swing.) Afternoon baseball — Wrigley Field has no lights — both prolonged his career and gave him an edge as a hitter. And the constant wind at Wrigley did not hurt him, either. Critics of Banks, mild and as few as they are, seem to dwell on the Wrigley wind. But if he has been helped by it, it is also true that he has more than once conquered the wind with long home runs that soared into what — his fans say — were hurricanes blowing in from Waveland Avenue. Ernie says simply: "Some you win, some you lose. That's the way the wind blows."

His performance aside, the impressive facet of Banks has been his implacability, his unruffled calm in the face of utter futility and embarrassment. Playing for the Cubs was like doing 10 to 20 at Folsom; a fine season for them was one in which they flirted with mediocrity. In an atmosphere such as this it is hard for a player — even if he is Ernie Banks — to retain his identity, to feel that he is of value when after the first two months of the season his club is so far off the pace that nothing seems of value. All that remains for the player, then, is four long, hot months in which the days stretch into other days to the point when on one muggy August afternoon in St. Louis he will stop and wonder — if he hasn't a thousand times before — what the hell he is doing there and sharply sense the silliness and vacuity of it all.

The milieu in Chicago was all of this and more, a Sahara of baseball where the emptiness was relieved only by Banks or by Phil Wrigley's nightmare boffo, the rotating coaching system. An abacus is necessary to tabulate the number of people Banks played under. All of them came, stayed for a cup of coffee and left as if they were walking in their sleep. Confronted by a parade of emotions, personalities, techniques and desperation, Banks remained Banks. His deportment never tottered amid the chaos, and he gave Chicago what he had, foot down on the gas, every day. He veered away from club politics, and he seemed to play a private game in his own little corner, never stopping to ponder how insignificant he might be or becoming sullen over the fact that all he could look toward each season was a lonely war with those dreadful figures.

The ballplayer's life is compressed in two or three hours each day, during which time he is under a microscope. Everything he does is picked apart. The manager might recognize his subtle contributions, his undramatic abilities that help a club win, but the front office — with few exceptions — leans on the figures for evaluation. Across a season, statistics hang above players like a canopy of gnats. He fears them more than injury, curses them more than the fatigue in his bones. They mean failure, and slowly over the years they leave their little scars on a ballplayer. He becomes suspicious, reticent, sometimes rude, sometimes paranoid.

"They are the worst things about the game," says Banks. "They are on a player's mind all the time. He eats them and sleeps with them, and they never let him alone. They change a man. But the figures lie. Sure, I've thought about them, but baseball, being a Cub, has always been fun. Fun, fun!"

Says one baseball man: "For a long time I used to think he was just a fantastic put-on. I mean, no sane person could be the way Banks was around the Cubs all those years. But now, you know, I think it's all real with him. If it isn't, he's certainly an extremely clever man."

Banks was born in Dallas, one of 12 children. His father picked cotton for a time and then became a stock clerk. As a boy Ernie shined shoes on the street, mowed lawns and tried cotton picking, but his father says, "Ernie never learned how to pick it. In fact the only work he ever did was at a hotel. He was supposed to carry out the garbage, but the cans were too heavy. After five days he quit and didn't even go back to collect his money." Banks' interest in baseball, which was slow in developing, grew intense in high school, and when he graduated he was signed by the Kansas City Monarchs, a Negro-league team that traveled in a bus that coughed its way to a different town each night. Tom Baird, the owner of the Monarchs, did not seem particularly high on Banks, but major league scouts soon were.

"I first heard of him from Bill Norman," says Bill Veeck, who then owned the St. Louis Browns. "He called me up and said, 'There's a kid here you gotta get. Best-lookin' thing I've ever seen.' So I got hold of Baird and asked him how much he wanted. He said $35,000. I told him I'd call him back. Then I called this banker. I already owed him my life. How about $35,000, I asked him? He said I already owed him my life. So what, I said, this kid is so great we'll all get even. The banker said he did not want to get even that much. I called Baird again and asked him if I could put $3,500 down, and I'd give him the balance when he found me. Baird said the trouble was that he could never find me. All right, I said, do me one favor, Tom. Don't sell him to anyone in the American League. I have enough troubles without another one. I then called up Jim Gallagher and put the Cubs on Banks."

Any other player would have had a gangster's contract out on Veeck in response to his gesture, but certainly not the grateful Banks, who joined the Cubs in September 1953. He arrived at Wrigley without a glove or a florin of his $35,000 selling price. He was lent a glove and given a book called *How to Play Baseball* by one of the Cub coaches. Banks threw the book away and went on to become a Chicago institution, right up there with Mayor Daley and George Halas. The scope of his appeal was illustrated two years ago when a massive sculpture by Picasso was unveiled. An alderman named John Hoellen described the work as a "rusting junk heap" and suggested that it be dismantled and a 50-foot statue of Ernie Banks — that symbol of a "vibrant city" — put in its place.

The only time Chicago has ever rejected Banks — aside from vocal anxiety that his career was at an end in the early '60s — was when he ran for alderman in the Eighth Ward, three miles from Comiskey Park. An independent Republican, Banks conducted an energetic campaign, and he did not miss a utopian base: lower taxes, safe streets, additional libraries, youth recreation, prompt garbage pick-ups and, as usual, a pennant in Wrigley Field. Mayor Daley, a White Sox fan, did not support him. The voters ignored him, too. Maybe, one guessed, it was his theme: "Put a slugger into city hall." The word "slugger" might have made too many people think of slugs; city hall was always notorious for slugs. At any rate, he lost, finishing third in a four-man race. He was not visibly disturbed. How could a Cub, he rationalized, get elected in Comiskey country?

Still, Banks' political ambitions are far from dampened. This August, Governor Richard Ogilvie appointed him to a $15,000-a-year position on the board of the Chicago Transit Authority. The appointment moved the governor's critics to suggest that he is a man of inestimable vision. Besides being a lure to Cub fans, Banks would be an inspiration in the black areas when Ogilvie seeks reelection. Perhaps, but Banks does not appear to have much clout among the blacks. His lack of militancy bugs them but, more important, they feel he is not a part of The Cause. Much of it has to do with his behavior or stance, which they think is that of a hat-in-hand old retainer. He is, too, a handy target for all their frustrations. They see in him all the mortgages that they have a difficult time acquiring, all the cabs that pass them by in their neighborhoods, all the little deaths in their lives.

"I don't agree with that thinking," says one black man. "How can Banks be an Uncle Tom? Why, he's never even been a Negro."

Maybe only a black man can sense what another black man is genuinely all about, but the attitude toward Banks appears to be somewhat harsh. Among his own, he occupies a lonely, pressurized position. He is, perhaps, too saccharine amid the maelstrom of social calamities, but he does not know any other way to be. "I care deeply about my people," says Banks, "but I'm just not one to go about screaming over what I contribute. I'm not black or white. I'm just a human being trying to survive the only way I know how. I don't make enemies. If I'm not crazy about somebody he'll never know it. I kill him with kindness." His latest manager, Leo Durocher, for one, might agree with that.

The union between Durocher and Banks, which began in 1966, was that in name only. Their disparate attitudes and personalities promised sudden conflict. Durocher was abrasive, insensitive and insistent on maximum competitiveness. Banks was placid, a baseball flower child and a power hitter who must hit to help a club; he has never been bold or much more than mediocre on the bases. Compounding the situation was the reputation that Ernie had. To the press and everyone else, he was Mr. Cub, a title that Leo seemed to resent. In his first spring training with the Cubs, Durocher made his move. He was certain that Banks was just another aging player, and he spent the entire training period using other players at first base. "I wish you'd knock off that Mr. Cub stuff," Leo finally told the press.

But it became evident that Leo's ploy was not going to work. The players he tried in Banks' position were either injured or failed to hit, but he still did not use Banks until shortly before Opening Day. The shock of not seeing Banks in the lineup may have even jolted Durocher, who decided to allow Banks to play himself out of the lineup. Banks never did, and he was a vital figure in the Cubs' climb to respectability. "The one reason why the Cubs are in the first division," Walter Alston said in 1967, "is Ernie Banks." The feeling now is that Durocher and Banks just tolerate each other. Banks is not enamored of Leo, and Leo is certainly not effusive in his praise of Banks. "I remember the time," says a reporter, "when Banks belted a pair of rooftop homers, and I went to the clubhouse. I said to Leo, 'He sure is some kind of ballplayer.' Leo said, 'He sure is. That Beckert [Glenn] is really something.' Beckert had done nothing exceptional that day." Banks, on the other hand, is always shrewdly generous to Durocher.

"I'm watching Ernie on this interview one day," says Bob Kennedy, one of Banks' former managers, "and suddenly from out of nowhere he says, 'Leo Durocher is the greatest manager I've ever seen.'" Laughing, Kennedy adds, "He's incredible. He's beautiful. Can you imagine him saying that about Leo?"

Well, yes, because that's Ernie Banks. "When Ernie dies," says one player, "and the undertaker is finished, he'll rise up and say, 'Nice job, buddy.'" He is one of a kind, a bit unctuous, maybe, and a bit too out of place in the year 1969, but he is, one guesses, more of a private person than many think. He is certainly the antithesis of the other Negro superstars, the silent Henry Aaron, the serious Willie Mays, the combative Jackie Robinson and the suspicious Bob Gibson. Soft colors, better than words, could perhaps define him. The wispy tempera of Andrew Wyeth might catch his gladness, his singularity, what he has that embodies a time in baseball that is no more, or maybe never was.

Raymond Coffey

Billy Williams Is In: That's What Really Counts This Week

Chicago Tribune, January 16, 1987

Forget the rest of it: the mayoral campaign, the Iran business, the rocketing stock market, the diving dollar, the Bears' flop, the weather forecast, all of it.

Billy Williams is moving into baseball's Hall of Fame, which is what really counts this week.

Justice is done, which unfortunately is not always a sure thing. The good guy won. The sun does shine. The good old days were the good old days.

The Cubs' great outfielder, old No. 26, the "Sweet Swinger" from Whistler, Ala., has all the numbers entitling him to join the immortals at Cooperstown — 426 home runs, a career .290 batting average over 18 seasons, National League rookie of the year in 1961, the batting champion [.333 with 37 homers] in 1972, an iron man who played in a then-record 1,117 games.

He was a ballplayer. He belongs in the Hall of Fame.

But Williams was more than a ballplayer, which is why he remains in, and belongs in, our memories.

The sporting world, like the rest of the world, seems overpopulated these days with knuckleheads and hot dogs and drug users and million-dollar loafers and coasters and people who don't try and who don't deliver and who make too much noise.

Not Billy Williams. Never. Ever. He came to work and he did his job and he never complained and he never got paid more than $150,000 a season.

He wasn't on TV selling tacos and tires and he wasn't in the newspapers demanding to have his contract renegotiated or second-guessing the manager.

He wasn't hanging out in the saloons or turning up in the gossip columns, either. He went fishing.

And he just kept going to the ballpark, coming up to bat and making life miserable for pitchers with that picture-perfect swing from the left side of the plate, and pulling fly balls out of the vines at Wrigley Field.

He played on mostly lousy teams, which seems to be the destiny of any Cub, and, like Hall of Fame teammate Ernie Banks, he never got to the World Series, which is a shame, and which is also one of the great disappointments of his life.

Because he played on mostly also-ran teams, because he never sought publicity or celebrity, because he was the kind of guy he is, Williams never got much attention from anyone but the Cubs' faithful.

Flamboyance, in the Reggie Jackson style, was never Williams' style. He'd have been embarrassed by those hot-dogging, high-fiving antics of the Mets last season.

He didn't go in for things like attention-getting headbands and goofy haircuts and getting out of shape and elbowing his way to the TV cameras.

He was, instead, as someone observed this week, the "Quiet Hero." About the only thing he ever got his name in the newspapers for was winning a game with his bat or saving a game with his glove, as he did for Ken Holtzman's no-hitter in 1969.

His old pal Banks was quoted this week as remembering that "Billy had a saying, 'When fish open their mouths, they get caught.' Billy didn't talk much. Billy just played."

But the Wrigley Field faithful know a ballplayer when they see one, maybe because they have seen so few of them in Cubs' uniforms, and they loved Billy Williams.

Williams, who retired in 1976, didn't make it into the Hall of Fame until his sixth year on the ballot. He missed by only four votes last year. It was a tough wait. But, typically, Billy Williams did his waiting quietly.

"Oh, that's really beautiful," he said when the call finally came this week that he was in. "Beautiful. Beautiful. Lovely. It was a long wait but it was worth it."

That was a long speech for Billy Williams. But, yes, it was beautiful. And it was worth waiting for.

It made our day — as Billy Williams used to make a lot of our days. Great ballplayer. Great man. Great memories.

Forget the rest of it. Time enough to go back to the world next week.

Mike Downey

He Throws a Wild Card into Game

Los Angeles Times, 1989

Wild Thing Williams, a combination of Dizzy Dean and Daffy Duck, hop-scotched through the Wrigley Field dugout Tuesday and then sprang up the steps — shaggy hair protruding from his cap, Cap'n Ahab beard fuzzing up his chin — until he whooshed right by the Chicago Cubs' last Hall of Famer, Billy Williams, whose specialties as a player were reliability and restraint. Cub careers are all these Williamses have ever had in common, trust us.

"All right, everybody watch your lips! I'm getting loose!" Mitch Williams cried out, to nobody in particular, for no particular reason, and then off he went to chuck some baseballs.

Billy Williams watched him come and go, shaking his head.

"Wiiiiild thing," he said.

Keep an eye on this deliverer of comic relief, this designated mad hatter, as the Cubs go after their first National League pennant in 44 years, starting tonight.

This is the character who, in his first season with the team, came within one save of Bruce Sutter's club record, but simultaneously became the relief pitcher Cub fans could and couldn't trust. Maybe he'd hit Harry Caray in the head. They never knew.

Wild Thing. He makes their hearts sing. He makes everything, well, groovy.

Cub pitcher Rick Sutcliffe, on Mitch Williams: "I pitch like I'm sitting in an easy chair, and he pitches like his hair's on fire."

Pittsburgh outfielder Andy Van Slyke, on Mitch Williams: "If everybody pitched like him, I'd quit."

He is the guy who makes Chicago heartbeats flutter like a knuckleball. Not only do the Cubs have Ryne Sandberg, they also have the second coming of Ryne Duren. One Mitch pitch goes down the pipe. Next Mitch pitch goes up the screen. Third Mitch pitch goes across the corner. Fourth Mitch pitch goes around the corner, out a side exit and into Yum-Yum Donuts, next door to Wrigley.

Wild Thing. They think they love him, but want to know for sure.

Cub fans could hardly believe their eyes when the man who cost them sweet-swinging Rafael Palmeiro in a nine-player trade toed the rubber on opening day, proceeded to walk the bases loaded, then proceeded to strike out the side. That, some will tell you, was his most consistent performance of the season. That was Mitch Williams on a *good* day.

Sometimes it's hard to tell a Mitch Williams pitch from a pickoff attempt.

"I'm not even invited to pitcher-catcher meetings before games anymore," Wild Thing said Tuesday, on the eve of the Cub playoff series against the San Francisco Giants. "They don't want to say anything to me because they don't want me thinking."

When he isn't pitching without thinking, Wild Thing is speaking without thinking. Or else it just comes out funny. Williams might get into hot water with some of his teammates if some of his quotes are taken out of context, condensed into one or two sentences, with all the true meaning and flavor sacrificed.

For example, while discussing Manager Don Zimmer's occasionally unorthodox strategy Tuesday, Wild Thing said:

"He makes certain moves and a lot of people look at him like he's got spinach in his teeth."

What you have to understand is the amount of admiration and affection Williams has for Zimmer, and that he wouldn't for all the world want to sound unkind to him.

This is the same way he feels toward shortstop Shawon Dunston, so when Williams says "some of the things he does on the basepaths are almost ignorant," the truth of the matter is that he is flattering Dunston, talking about how his teammate is so unbelievably aggressive that opponents can't believe how crazy his baserunning is.

They feel much the same way about Williams' pitching. Everybody does. They call him Wild Thing because he is definitely a wildman, and because actor Charlie Sheen played a character with that nickname in a baseball comedy. But they also call for him whenever the Cubs need a couple of outs in the ninth inning.

"I don't particularly care what I'm called, as long as they keep calling," Williams said. "As long as they're calling me something other than 'bum.'"

What makes Mitch pitch? What can be expected of him from one day to the next? Almost anything. One day in Pittsburgh, he took a Jeff King line drive in the temple. Next day, he pitched. Teammates kidded him that the ball hit him in the one place no damage could be done.

This is a franchise that at various times has had its hands on Sutter, Lee Smith, Guillermo (Willie) Hernandez, Goose Gossage, Bill Caudill, the late Donnie Moore, even the ace of the Giant bullpen that opposes them in this series, Craig Lefferts, and often was left agonizing as these relievers carried other franchises into the playoffs. Last time the Cubs won a World Series, in 1908, was there even such a thing as a "relief pitcher?"

Now, here's this goofball with a fastball, Wild Thing Williams, who spends his spare time at bowling alleys, and gets his lower torso tattooed, and avoids the barber the way some people avoid the dentist, and today it might be up to him whether Chicago goes most of the 20th Century without a baseball championship, North Side or South.

Babe Ruth once pointed toward center field here before swinging. Perhaps Mitch Williams will point toward the press box before throwing. Anytime he doesn't kill anybody this series, they ought to give him a save.

THE FAITHFUL

Perhaps no adjective in the English language has become more annoyingly affixed to a noun than has "long-suffering" to "Cub fans." The implication seems to be that there is something masochistic or existentially pathetic about being devoted to the Cubs. True Cub lovers prefer to think that their dauntless loyalty to the team is a sign not of neurosis or metaphysical anomie, but of a far nobler human attribute: *character*. Mets fans and other cynics never hesitate to point out (with a certain perverse glee, I think) that the "character" argument is nothing but a rationalization for continuing to follow a losing team. But they wouldn't know, because they have no character. Thus, we close with a diverse collection of musings by and about the Cub faithful, none of whom would likely admit to any particular proclivity for pain.

Our first three writers plumb the psychological depths of being a Cub fan — Jim Langford from three personal angles, George Will with his trademark philosophical overview, and Harry Stein from the perspective of an outsider. Then Roy Blount, Jr., offers a loopy account of his real-life indulgence of every Bruin Backer's dream: to take the field with the Boys in Blue. Bernie Lincicome makes a convincing case for saving a spot on the bandwagon for himself and his fellow Johnny-come-latelies. Before meeting the fictional Bleacher Bums, Lonnie Wheeler introduces us to the real thing with his account of the opening of the 1987 season, when he spent the entire summer in the Wrigley Field bleachers. Those maniacal denizens of the cheap seats were immortalized in the Organic Theater hit play, *Bleacher Bums*, of which we gladly provide an excerpt. Melancholy notes are sounded by Gordon Edes, who recounts the untimely death of songwriter/Cub fan Steve Goodman, and Mike Downey, with his tart postmortem on the Boys of Zimmer. And the last word goes to Jon Margolis, who pauses on the eve of the '89 playoffs to wonder aloud if Cub fans might not be better off now than they would be if the 45-year drought were to come to an end.

Jim Langford

On Being a Cub Fan

The Game Is Never Over: An Appreciative History
of the Chicago Cubs

We are dealing here with a mystery: why would anyone of
sound mind continue to love a team that has not only not won
a pennant for thirty-four years, but which has done more
depth-diving than the German U-boat force in World War II.
Rooting for the Cubs is like continuing to fly on Disaster
Airlines, Inc., with a record of at least one major crash every
year; you have to be an incredible optimist, a complete pessimist, or a candidate for *The Guinness Book of World Records*
in the category of stoicism in the face of interminable adver-
sity.

I cannot solve the mystery. The best I can do is to make
public a memo I wrote my two boys on what baseball means
to me, then to invent a conversation with a psychiatrist on
what led me to be a Cub fan, and finally to share with you
letters I have written over the past thirty years to P. K.
Wrigley and his son William Wrigley.

I

Memo to: Jeremy and Joshua
From: Dad
Subject: Baseball
Dear Sons:

As you know, the snow is melting and before long we will again experience spring. Little pieces are beginning to appear in the back of the sports page notifying us that spring training camps are open; the next breeze that comes from the south will bring with it the crisp crack of baseballs against leather and wood. It is time for us to oil our own gloves. Soon we'll be tossing the ball, playing hotbox, and I'll be throwing you my split-fingered fast ball with the house as our catcher-backstop. Since we use a tennis ball and since the neighbors have a picture window in straightaway center field, I will again attempt to make you pull the ball to the blue spruce in left. Remember, the pin oak in right is an automatic out. I should warn you that I intend to mix up my pitches this year. I am a year older now and my legs and arm are not as strong as they were last year.

The onset of spring will require a few adjustments in our routine and priorities. While I really did enjoy playing Nerf football and basketball with you, from now until October if that is what you want to play you'll have to do without me. I cannot be Roger Staubach and Bruce Sutter at the same time. What I am trying to say is that baseball will take precedence over other activities in the months ahead. I will be needing more time to study the sports page. In the evenings when the Cubs are on the road, the television is hereby reserved. Besides, you probably watch too much television anyway.

I hope that you will want to watch a lot of games with me. I will get you to Wrigley Field in person as often as I can. It pleases me very much that you like baseball. Let me tell you why.

Baseball is very much like life. Watch it closely, and you will learn a great deal about things like courage, beauty,

strength, finesse, chance, fallibility, and loyalty. Study baseball and you will have a head start in understanding life. Even
at your ages, you've rallied in the late innings and turned
defeat into victory. You also know what it is like to lose
suddenly with one mistake what it had taken time and energy
to build. You have schoolmates whose scrappiness lifts them
above their ordinary talents. And you know others who could
do a lot better than they are doing but who don't seem to
care. There are a lot of baseball players of both types. And
there are many who are very talented and who develop their
skills to the full by giving all they have all the time. You will
see rookies whose agility allows them to challenge established players for a regular spot in the lineup. But note how
cagey veterans use experience and know-how to fend off
such a challenge, at least for another year. It is right that
Young Turks attempt to take over from their elders, but
strength alone cannot displace wisdom.

Let your imagination run free. Fantasize yourself into
games. Be the left fielder who makes a spectacular leaping
catch at the wall to save the game . . . but sometimes imagine
yourself as the hitter who gave it all he had only to be denied
by that catch. Like some players, you will have days in your
life when you make two errors on the same play; remember,
there is always a chance for redemption. I've seen lots of
players change boos to cheers with one swing of the bat.

In baseball as in life, there are advances and setbacks.
Even in the midst of a losing streak, there is assurance that,
if we keep working at it, someday soon there will again be
cause for joy. And winning streaks too must end.

Baseball is not as simple as it looks. Every game presents
a huge variety of possibilities that have to be weighed by the
manager and coaches. At the heart of it all is the ability to
take calculated risks. On every pitch there is strategy in
operation: the guessing game between pitcher and hitter,
where the fielders position themselves, who will cover which
base, how the wind is blowing, who is next in the batting
order, who to warm up in the bullpen and when to bring him

in. All of this goes on simultaneously, almost instinctively, and the fan is challenged to capture all or even part of it in one eyebite.

It is good to learn that even the best laid plans can run afoul of chance and circumstance. You'll see easy grounders elude fielders by hitting a pebble in the infield, you'll watch home runs blown into long foul balls by a sudden gust of wind, and you will see games won or lost because of a checked-swing hit or the mistaken call of an umpire. There are things in life that happen like that too. The best we can do is to rebound from them with grace.

Baseball is a game of exquisite moves, of subtlety no less demanding than that of a concert orchestra. It is a thrilling sight to watch the pitching motion of a Steve Carlton, the swing of a Billy Williams or Rod Carew, the incredible fielding of a Brooks Robinson or Graig Nettles, the strong beautiful throw from a rightfielder like Roberto Clemente that cuts down a runner at the plate. Beauty is where you find it. You can even find it at Wrigley Field.

Courage, anger, exhaustion, and exuberance are part of every game, as they are of every life. If you study the records, you will discover that individual stars may dominate a team, but team play as a whole is the crucial factor in the final standings. No team has ever won a pennant without good utility players.

Finally, be gentle in your judgment of the Cubs. It does us no credit to complain about our players because they are not as good as those fielded by other teams. Our protest must be directed toward the management, which either thinks that these guys are really good or that we won't care if they're not.

At your age, Jeremy, I became addicted to baseball and to the Cubs. I used to race home from school at 2:45 so that I could listen to the last few innings of the Cubs. As soon as the radio warmed up, there would be Bert Wilson describing the scene and I could tell by the tone of his voice after only a few words whether we were ahead or behind. For my eleventh birthday in June, my father gave me the *Complete*

Encyclopedia of Baseball, a book I still treasure despite its vintage. There I studied and learned the past glories of the Cubs, though they now floundered at the bottom of the League. If you think Cub fans have it bad now, you should have followed the 1948 version. We had an infield like a fishnet. Roy Smalley at shortstop and Andy Pafko — who was made to play third though he was a fine outfielder — led the league in errors at their respective positions. And somebody named Dutch McCall was 4–13 on the mound that year. But from that season on I have never wavered even momentarily in my devotion to the Cubs. As Bert Wilson used to repeat time and again with two outs in the ninth and the Cubs trailing by half-a-dozen runs, "The game is never over until the last man is out." The game has never been over for me. It goes on through the winter until it takes up where it left off the previous season. Baseball is a celebration of hope. Maybe that's why the season begins in the spring.

II

Not even my psychiatrist questions my love for baseball. The last time I saw him I used some analogies from the game to explain how optimism is so important to my outlook on life. The next thing I knew, he wanted to go into specifics.

"What team do you follow?" he asks.

"The Cubs," I say with no hint of apology or embarrassment.

"Umhummm," he responds, "And how do you feel about liking the Cubs?"

"How do I feel about it? Well, great, I guess."

"Great?"

"WHY do you like the CUBS?"

"You mean, 'Why do I LOVE the Cubs?'"

"All right."

"Well, they might be a little weak at second, and they need two starting pitchers and another outfielder, but. . . ."

"No, that's not what I'm asking you. I want to know how

anyone, particularly someone with at least a modicum of intelligence, can give this kind of devotion to a team that hasn't won a pennant for thirty-four years. And that's putting it as gently as I can."

"O.K., I see. I'll tell you why. It's because of Bert Wilson, Jack Quinlan, Milo Hamilton, Jack Brickhouse, Vince Lloyd, Lou Boudreau. . . ."

"Were these childhood friends of yours?"

"In a way. They were the voices I grew up with. They were the people who were on the scene; they taught me to love the Cubs no matter what."

"You heard voices . . . where were these voices coming from?"

"WIND, WGN, from all the cities in the National League and especially from Beautiful Wrigley Field."

"And what did these voices say?"

"I'll tell you what they said. Bert Wilson said that the Cubs were a wonderful team, beleaguered by bad luck, victims of circumstances, but always ready for more, always building, always about to reach their full potential, always trying. Bert taught me to believe that even if you're behind 16–0 with two outs in the ninth, there is still a chance. He was right, you know, the game isn't over until the last man is out. Jack Quinlan, Milo Hamilton, and Vince Lloyd were cut from the same cloth. They make Tug McGraw look like a plagiarist. And Jack Brickhouse taught me how to survive defeat. I mean even if we got drubbed, Jack would appear in the post-game show completely unshaken. He'd tell us not to worry, that every team has a bad day and now that we have that out of our system we can look forward to tomorrow. If it was a narrow loss, Jack would point out how close it was and how with a minor change of wind velocity at the right moment we could have won it. If we won, Jack would remind us how well our boys played, how good they are looking now, and he'd get us ready for a winning streak. The thing is, you could believe Jack Brickhouse; you could tell he meant what he said. And Jack had been doing this for twenty-five years, so he knew what he was talking about. And from Lou Boudreau I learned how easy it is to mispronounce names. For example, he always called Len Gabrielson 'Len Gableson.' But so what? Lou's in the Hall of Fame. He knows a lot about baseball.

"I mean I was raised on these voices. I remember days in the summer when my Dad had the radio tuned to Bob Elson reciting the woes of the White Sox, and I'd stay for a laugh or two and then go outside where the sky was perfectly blue and the leaves were blowing gently on the trees that lined our street. Our neighbor would be washing his car, and he'd have the Cubs game playing on his radio, and I'd sit on his steps and pet his dog 'Boots' and root for the Cubs."

The psychiatrist took off his glasses and rubbed his eyes. He interrupted me, "That's all very nice. But surely as you grew older, you realized that there were better teams to follow."

"Hey, wait a minute! Sure there were better teams; but not worth giving up the Cubs for. Listen, it doesn't take any courage to be a Yankee or Dodger fan."

"I know, but I assume you know that of the sixteen teams in existence in 1948, all of them have won at least one pennant since then except for the Cubs. Do you regard yourself as a pessimist? Do you like pain?"

"A pessimist! I'm a fanatic optimist. If Bert, Jack, Vince, Milo, Jack, Lou, and I were locked in a stable piled to the roof with horse droppings, we'd all start digging to find the pony. No! I don't LIKE pain. Being a Cubs fan has helped me see past pain. Look. Suppose the Cubs are leading three to nothing in the ninth inning. Let's say that our pitcher slips off the mound as he is warming up and sprains his ankle. So we bring in, oh, say, Paul Reuschel. The Phillies get three hits in a row, and now it's 3–1 with runners on first and third. We bring in Willie Hernandez, and he strikes out two batters. But the next one singles, and it's 3–2. Then Ontiveros drops a foul fly, and Schmidt hits Willie's next pitch into Waveland Avenue and we lose 5–3. I'm not going to slam the television and storm around like some Yankee fan. Jack Brickhouse's 'oh, brother' when Schmidt swings and connects is all the comment that's needed. If Ontiveros catches that pop foul, we win. So Ontiveros makes a mistake. Do you want me to hold that against him? We all make mistakes."

"Well, maybe the explanation is that you just have very low expectations for the Cubs, and that's why it doesn't bother you when they lose."

"Wrong again, Doc. How can I have low expectations? Every game is different. There is always a chance. Season averages don't always tell the whole story. I've seen .300 hitters strike out in crucial situations and .167 hitters win games. It's like Vince Lloyd always says, 'Anyone with a bat in his hands is dangerous.'"

"All right. But be honest with me. Haven't you ever been tempted way down inside to abandon the Cubs for a more exciting team. . . . Look at the Cardinals, you could have been cheering for Musial, Slaughter, Gibson. . . ."

The passion with which he spoke alerted me to the fact that beneath the horned rim glasses and the cool, calm exterior, my shrink was a Cardinal fan. I decided to take him on. "Well," I said aggressively, "if the Cardinals are so great, why have the Cubs whipped them in a majority of series over the past twenty years?"

His eyes lit up with a fiendish flash that betrayed his loss of professional composure. "Well," he asked with a banzai tone in his voice, "THEN HOW THE HELL DO YOU FEEL ABOUT THE BROCK-FOR-BROGLIO TRADE?"

Then I knew I had him. He'd gone for the jugular. He thought he had me with two outs in the ninth and nobody on. I paused. Bert's words came back, "The game is never over until the last man is out." I looked at him calmly, like Jack Brickhouse would. "You know something, Doc? The same team that traded Brock for Broglio went on to trade Larry Jackson and Bob Buhl at the end of their careers to the Phillies for Fergie Jenkins, Adolfo Phillips, and John Herrnstein, and after getting six straight 20-game years out of Jenkins, traded him to Texas for Bill Madlock who won two straight batting titles. Besides, Billy Williams was a better left fielder than Brock anyway!"

He was stunned. We both knew that a shift had taken place. Shaken, he said that we will do a little word association and call it a day.

"Mediocrity," he said nastily.

"Improvement," I replied suavely.

"Last place," he spat.

"Mets," I retorted quickly.

"Error," he snorted.

"Smalley," I said before thinking, but, recovering quickly, I added, "Forgive."

"Hopeless," he snapped.

"Never."

"Losers."

"Wait till next year," I said.

"My bill," he cried in resignation.

"Wait till next year."

III

September 1, 1948

Mr. P. K. Wrigley
Wrigley Field
Chicago, Ill.
Dear Mr. Wrigley:

I read your ad in the paper apologizing for the 1948 Cubs. I am just eleven years old and I don't know what the answer is, but don't blame the players. Bert Wilson said that they are trying as hard as they can. Maybe we need new players. Why don't you hire Branch Rickey away from the Dodgers and give him the money he needs to build a better team? (Well, what do I know? I'm just a kid.)

Your Friend,
Jim Langford

January 15, 1950

Mr. P. K. Wrigley
Wrigley Field
Chicago, Ill.
Dear Mr. Wrigley:

Remember me? I'm thirteen now and two years ago I wrote you and suggested that you hire Branch Rickey. I saw in the paper that you hired Mr. Wid Matthews who worked for Mr. Rickey. I still wish you'd gotten Mr. Rickey himself but maybe Mr. Matthews will be good. I wrote to Frankie Frisch applying for a job as a bat boy but he never answered. I wrote to Hank Sauer and told him how glad I am that he is a Cub. He wrote me back a real nice letter. Why don't you make Hank Sauer manager?

Sincerely,
Jim Langford

October 13, 1951

Mr. P. K. Wrigley
Wrigley Field
Chicago, Ill.
Dear Mr. Wrigley:

Do you think there is any possibility that Wid Matthews is getting a kickback from Branch Rickey? Trading Andy Pafko to the Dodgers makes Roy Smalley look flawless by comparison. And since you probably sign the checks, you've probably noticed how much he is spending to buy up leftovers from the Dodger system.

I'm glad that Frankie Frisch has been fired and that you're going to keep Phil Cavarretta for another year as manager. Old number 44 is great and if he can't do it I don't know who can.

As Always,
Jim Langford

April 3, 1956

Mr. P. K. Wrigley
Wrigley Field
Chicago, Ill.

Dear Mr. Wrigley:

How are you? I want you to know that I think you're getting a bum rap from the press. They say you care more about gum than you do about the Cubs. That isn't true. Surely you've suffered even more than we have. You impress me as a highly principled man. I mean, anyone who refuses to yield to the lure of increased attendance that comes with night baseball because you don't want to disturb the neighborhood around your park is somebody special. I'll bet you're even tempted to feel guilty about taking our money at the box office. Don't. We love the Cubs.

I do want to share a few thoughts with you, and since I have been writing to you for eight years, I hope you won't mind if I say what I really think.

The thing is, we are now in the seventh year of Wid Matthews' Five-Year Plan, and things look pretty bad. The fact that he just traded Hank Sauer for Pete Whisenant and $10,000 is not redeemed even by his success in getting rid of Roy Smalley.

Like you, I hoped it would work to trade a lot and to have Cubs from the last pennant team come back as managers. I think you made a big mistake in firing Phil Cavarretta, though I'm sure that Stan Hack is a nice guy. But it wouldn't be a mistake to fire Matthews. Let him go back to work for Branch Rickey; Rickey owes him one (or maybe fifteen!). Meanwhile, maybe you could see if Frank Lane would be interested in the job. What do you think?

Devotedly,
Jim

October 11, 1962

Mr. P. K. Wrigley
Wrigley Field
Chicago, Ill.
Dear Mr. Wrigley:

I've written you, off and on, for fourteen years. While I applaud many of the innovations you have hatched during that time to strengthen the Cubs, I'm afraid that the latest one is proving to be a disaster of rather major proportions. The Cubs have been like the Spanish army on San Juan Hill trying to find their leaders to fend off Teddy Roosevelt's attack.

Years ago, you suggested installing a punching bag in the dressing room so that the players could work off their tensions and be relaxed at game time. How were you to know that they would take the field in such a placid manner? Then you paid for a deluxe pitching machine to help the boys in spring training. Too bad you couldn't have dressed the machine and started it on opening day. A few seasons ago you ordered an oxygen bottle for the dugout. It was not your fault that the only person who used it was Pat Peiper, the field announcer. But your idea of revolving managers is a bust. In two seasons we've won 123 and lost 193, and not one of the revolvers has a winning record. It's bad enough when the players don't know whether or where they might play on any given day; it's worse when the manager pro tempore has to be concerned about whether he'll be able to get to O'Hare in time to catch the 4:45 flight to San Antonio. Why don't you take this occasion to set a new record by firing the whole bunch at once? I've been with you up to this point, but now you're pushing it a bit. For the next month, I'm going to chew Dentyne.

Sincerely,
Jim Langford

February 6, 1966

Mr. P. K. Wrigley
Wrigley Field
Chicago, Ill.
Dear Mr. Wrigley:

I am sure you are painfully aware that in the four years since the league expanded to ten teams, the Cubs have finished ninth once, seventh once, and eighth twice. Now you've hired Leo Durocher. Putting aside for a moment the fact that I don't like Durocher's style, I think I should warn you lest you put credence in his statements and make yourself vulnerable to further hurts. I remember back in 1951 when Durocher predicted big things for the Cubs. You will recall that they finished last. The next year he made a wisecrack about Hank Sauer. Hank, you will recall, won the Most Valuable Player in the league award that year. Now Durocher is quoted as saying that the Cubs are not an eighth place ballclub. Look out, Mr. Wrigley. Remember, there are ten places in the league now.

Yours,
Jim

August 3, 1969

Mr. P. K. Wrigley
Wrigley Field
Chicago, Ill.
Dear Mr. Wrigley:

You've done it! I'll have to admit that I didn't like Durocher and still don't. I think even I could have managed this team to the pennant. This has to be one of the greatest Cubs teams ever. We have power, fielding, good catching, and fine pitching. Wow! And a majority of the roster grew up in our farm system. Those who didn't came to us in fabulous trades: Jenkins, Phillips, and Herrnstein for Jackson and Buhl; Hands and Hundley for almost nothing! Sheer genius!

I'm not a season ticket-holder because I live in South Bend. Is there any way you can see that I get series tickets? Now that we are ten games ahead of the league, I'm sure the lines are already long. Wow! Finally! Let the Yankees eat their hearts out!

Congratulations,
Jim

August 21, 1972

Mr. P. K. Wrigley
Wrigley Field
Chicago, Ill.
Dear Mr. Wrigley:

It's been nearly a quarter of a century since I first wrote you and about three years since my last letter. I decided to wait a while after what happened in 1969; I know that you were even more disappointed than I was. If we didn't know the meaning of "swoon" before then, we sure learned it that September. What rotten luck! Maybe we need to look into exorcism as a possibility.

I'm glad Durocher is gone. But it looks to me like the Cubs of '69 are over the hill. Banks, Beckert, Kessinger, Santo, Williams, Hickman, Hundley, Jenkins, Hands . . . What a team! What a shame!

About twenty years ago you said that if one system doesn't work, we'll try another. By now we must be on system number eighteen. Let me offer you a suggestion. Why don't we break the mold of slow-footed sluggers, of pitching staffs built around one bona fide starter? Let's go after some guys who can scratch out hits and run like hell, guys who rob hitters with astonishing speed afield, and who show the kind of scrappiness that slides in head first. And let's get some thin, stylish pitchers. How about Maury Wills as manager? We've been at it for a long time, Mr. Wrigley, but speed's the one thing we haven't tried. If things don't improve, I may try some myself.

All best,
Jim

November 3, 1977

Mr. William Wrigley
Wrigley Field
Chicago, Ill.
Dear Mr. Wrigley:

I was genuinely grieved by your father's death. Although I never met him in person, I corresponded with him for many years, and I admired him very much. I don't think many people have done as much for baseball as your father did. Among many other things, it was largely through his efforts and initiative that major league baseball made it to the West Coast. Moreover, he always stood high as a man of fairness and principle. I only wish that the Cubs could have won a championship for him.

Now that you have taken over, I hope that they win a title for you. To be quite honest with you, I hope they win one for me before I die.

If you go through the files, you may come across letters I have written since 1948. I hope you won't mind if I continue to offer a suggestion now and then. I've spent a great deal of time trying to figure out what possible course of action could help us win.

Do we need more and better scouts?

Do we need to be more astute in our trades?

Do we need to concentrate on pitching, fielding, and speed?

Should we get into the free-agent market?

☒ All of the above.

Yours Sincerely,
James R. Langford

March 26, 1980

Mr. William Wrigley
Wrigley Field
Chicago, Ill.
Dear Mr. Wrigley:

I've got it! Eureka! I know how we can turn the Cubs into winners! You are no doubt aware that various minor leagues use a system whereby the season is divided into two equal halves. The team in first place after half the games are played is declared winner of the first half. The league starts even for the second half of the season. If a different team comes out on top in the second half, the winner of the first half and the winner of the second half play off for the championship.

Mr. Wrigley, lobby, fight, scratch, and cajole to get that system adopted in the major leagues. Tell Bowie Kuhn he'll have a chance to play major domo at all kinds of playoff games. He'll love it. So will Howard Cosell.

You see, don't you, that we've got an instant dynasty on this system? What team is always at or near the top in late June? Right, the Cubs. July, August, and September swoons won't matter anymore! We can do our thing — play over our heads for three months and then rest the next three months, giving rookies a chance to play until the playoffs begin. This will work! We're in!

Go get 'em.

Your friend,
Jim

George F. Will

The Chicago Cubs, Overdue

The Pursuit of Happiness and Other Sobering Thoughts

A reader demands to know how I contracted the infectious conservatism for which he plans to horsewhip me. So if you have tears, gentle reader, prepare to shed them now as I reveal how my gloomy temperament received its conservative warp from early and prolonged exposure to the Chicago Cubs.

The differences between conservatives and liberals are as much a matter of temperament as ideas. Liberals are temperamentally inclined to see the world as a harmonious carnival of sweetness and light, where goodwill prevails, good intentions are rewarded, the race is to the swift, and a benevolent Nature arranges a favorable balance of pleasure over pain. Conservatives (and Cub fans) know better.

Conservatives know the world is a dark and forbidding place where most new knowledge is false, most improvements are for the worse, the battle is not to the strong, nor riches to men of understanding, and an unscrupulous Providence consigns innocents to suffering. I learned this early.

Out in central Illinois, where men are men and I am native, in 1948, at age seven, I made a mad, fateful blunder. I fell ankle over elbows in love with the Cubs. Barely advanced beyond the bib-and-cradle stage, I plighted my troth to a baseball team destined to dash the cup of life's joy from my lips.

Spring, earth's renewal, a season of hope for the rest of mankind, became for me an experience comparable to being slapped around the mouth with a damp carp. Summer was like being bashed across the bridge of the nose with a crowbar — ninety times. My youth was like a long rainy Monday in Bayonne, New Jersey.

Each year the Cubs charged onto the field to challenge anew the theory that there are limits to the changes one can ring on pure imcompetence. By mid-April, when other kids' teams were girding for Homeric battles at the top of the league, my heroes had wilted like salted slugs and begun their gadarene descent to the bottom. By September they had set a mark for ineptness at which others — but not next year's Cubs — would shoot in vain.

Every litter must have its runt, but my Cubs were almost all runts. Topps baseball bubblegum cards always struggled to say something nice about each player. All they could say about the Cubs' infielder Eddie Miksis was that in 1951 he was tenth in the league in stolen bases, with eleven.

Like the boy who stood on the burning deck whence all but he had fled, I was loyal. And the downward trajectory of my life was set. An eight-year-old could not face these fires without being singed, unless he had the crust of an armadillo, and how many eight-year-olds do?

Of the sixteen teams that existed in 1949, all have since won league championships — all but the Cubs. And which of the old National League teams was first to finish in tenth place behind even the expansion teams? Don't ask. Since 1948 the Cubs have played more than 6,000 hours of losing baseball. My cruel addiction continued. In 1964 I chose to do three years of graduate study at Princeton because Princeton is midway between Philadelphia and New York — two National League cities. All I remember about my wedding day in 1967 is that the Cubs dropped a doubleheader.

Only a team named after baby bears would have a shortstop

named Smalley — a righthanded hitter, if that is the word for a man who in his best year (1953) hit .249. From Roy Smalley I learned the truth about the word "overdue." A portrait of this columnist as a tad would show him with an ear pressed against a radio, listening to an announcer say: "The Cubs have the bases loaded. If Smalley gets on, the tying run will be on deck. And Smalley is overdue for a hit."

It was the most consoling word in the language, "overdue." It meant: in the long run, everything is going to be all right. No one is really a .222 hitter. We are all good hitters, all winners. It is just that some of us are, well, "overdue" for a hit, or whatever.

Unfortunately, my father is a righthanded logician who knows more than it is nice to know about the theory of probability. With a lot of help from Smalley, he convinced me that Smalley was not "overdue." Stan Musial batting .249 was overdue for a hot streak. Smalley batting .249 was doing his best.

Smalley retired after eleven seasons with a lifetime average of .227. He was still overdue.

Now once again my trained senses tell me: spring is near. For most of the world hope, given up for dead, stirs in its winding linen. But I, like Figaro, laugh that I may not weep. Baseball season approaches. The weeds are about to reclaim the trellis of my life. For most fans, the saddest words of tongue or pen are: "Wait 'til next year." For us Cub fans, the saddest words are: "This is next year."

The heart has its reasons that the mind cannot refute, so I say:

Do not go gently into this season, Cub fans; rage, rage against the blasting of our hopes. Had I but world enough, and time, this slowness, Cubs, would be no crime. But I am almost halfway through my allotted three-score-and-ten and you, sirs, are overdue.

Harry Stein

A Visit to Wrigley —
Where Hope Springs Infernal

Sport Magazine, June 1983

Buried in the 1983 Chicago Cubs media guide, in a section entitled "A Look Back at 1982," is a thought that stops the first-time visitor to the Wrigley Field press box: "'If we could've stayed away from the 13-game and eight-game [losing] streaks,' manager Lee Elia said after the season, 'there's no telling what we could have accomplished.'"

The visitor reads the sentence over; then again. Then — he cannot help himself — he erupts in laughter.

The fellow beside him, a reporter with a Chicago radio station, glances at the visitor, then at the source of his mirth, and edges his seat a few inches away.

"Wait," says the visitor, "look at this." He indicates the passage. "Yeah, and if only the *Titanic* hadn't hit that iceberg, it would have been a terrific cruise."

The radio fellow nods. "Typical." A beat. "But it's true what Elia says."

The visitor should not, of course, be surprised. After all, for years he has heard about Cub fans, those odd souls in whom optimism and fatalism co-mingle in a fashion otherwise reserved for groupies of doomed political campaigns and the most forlorn denizens of racetracks; and he has, over the course of the previous couple of hours on opening day, 1983, personally run across enough examples of the breed to dispel any notion that the image might simply have been a media creation. He has consorted with them in hangouts like Leo's Dug Out and The Cubby Bear, atop a roof on Waveland Avenue overlooking the outfield, in the bleachers themselves, and never before, not on film nor in life, has he encountered so vivid a display of the love-hate syndrome in flower.

To be sure, every Cub diehard worth his salt is able to acknowledge the dimension of his malady, and even to make light of it. One plump fellow at The Bleachers bar claimed to have had the words "Chicago Cubs, Where the Sun Don't Shine" tattooed on his backside. But even in the jauntiest of fans, hope, that deceitful little bugger, continues to leap, lunge, shimmy eternal. "I can't wait 'til the Cubs take the Series," the fellow with the tattoo had added confidentially. "I plan to moon the whole damn country on TV."

Now, in the press box, the visitor slams shut his media guide and sighs. It can start to put a person on edge, this business of hanging around with the inmates. Happily, on the field below, frigid and windblown as the gulag, someone named Debbie Shapiro is sashaying up to a microphone to sing a couple of national anthems; the Expos are the Cubs' opening day rivals. Having done so, she elicits a roar from the crowd, beams toward the upper deck, waves with both hands — and is pelted in the face by rain.

An instant later, the umpires call out the grounds crew.

"Typical," mutters the radio guy. "Even God hates the damn Cubs."

In something akin to desperation, the visitor flees the press box. A mistake. Nine-tenths of the opening day throng, chased by the rain, has surged into the cavernous passage-ways, packing the interior of the stadium. The visitor finds himself slammed against a concrete abutment next to an aging gentleman who wears a huge button reading "The Cubs Will Shine in '69."

"I ain't seen a crowd like this since *Gandhi*," offers the old guy.

"Nice button," replies the visitor, warily. "A collector's item."

"I wear it as a reminder," he says. *"Never again.* Since '69, my heart has been closed to them fickle bums." He pauses, then adds, "Now I just come out for the enjoyment of the game."

"I thought the Cubs were incurable."

"No way. Remember the Cubs' song in '69 — 'Hey hey, holy mackerel, the Cubs are on their way'? Well, one day, as the Cubs were blowing it, I nearly put my hand through a jukebox." He taps his button. "Never again."

They fall silent. Beside them, two local youths, 14 or 15 years old, are loudly speculating as to how many individuals might be slain by a rifleman perched atop Wrigley's roof.

"You'd wipe out 100, at least," observes the one in the Cubs' cap.

"Maybe," replies his friend in the down jacket, "but some of 'em you wouldn't kill. You'd just wound 'em."

"Shouldn't you two be in school or someplace?" asks the old guy.

"What's it to you?" counters the down jacket.

The old guy shrugs and takes a bite of the hot dog he has been hoarding. "You know," he tells the visitor, "before the war, I didn't care for hot dogs. But after three years of spam and crackers and soluble coffee, I started to crave 'em."

Abruptly, the local youths are intrigued. "You were in the war?"

"Landed in France. D-Day plus six."

"You shoot anyone?"

The old guy laughs. "Me? I spent the war scrounging for eats."

For the next 45 minutes, the old guy entertains the kids with war stories, at the end of which something so like a sense of camaraderie has developed between them that he is moved to offer the pair a piece of advice: "Listen, don't skip school for the Cubs. They ain't worth the heartbreak."

"What are you talking about," argues the kid with the cap,

"they're on the way up. They got Cey and Hall and. . . ."

"Listen to some timeless wisdom," interrupts the old guy. "If Mel Hall has a good year, the Cubs'll finish fifth. If Mel Hall doesn't have a good year, the Cubs'll finish fifth."

"Don't argue with him, man," one kid says. "The guy's on a mission."

Before the discussion can proceed further, a message booms over the loudspeaker: the game has been called. The youngsters attach themselves to the mob making for the exit.

"Remember what I told you," shouts the old guy after them.

"Yeah, right," calls one. "See you tomorrow."

Moments later, the old guy too is on his way out. He says nothing, but as he shuffles along, almost imperceptibly, a smile begins to play on his lips — growing, finally, into a full-fledged grin.

"What's up?" asks the visitor. "Why are you smiling?"

"I ain't smiling." He hesitates. "Not a bad opening day, though, huh? At least they didn't lose."

Roy Blount, Jr.

We All Had a Ball

Sports Illustrated, February 21, 1983

I have a T-shirt and two sweat shirts that say "I PLAYED BASEBALL AGAINST THE 1969 CUBS." This intro lets me get on with the rest of the story. "Hello, my name is Blat, Blong, Bough — whatever, it doesn't matter — and the very fact that Ferguson Jenkins was playing me deep enough to catch a ball hit 350 feet tells you something" is how I usually begin.

"Excuse me?" people reply.

"I hit a ball 350 feet," I say.

"Where?"

"Pulled it dead to left. It was caught — over the shoulder, but still, he must have been playing me pretty deep — by Ferguson Jenkins. He was in left at the time. You know how guys over thirty-five are; they like to live out their fantasies, and Jenkins probably always wanted to rob a sportswriter of extra bases. Earlier in camp, he called me — just a minute, I think I have the exact wording somewhere . . . here it is: 'A good hitter.' O.K., you *could* say that's the kind of thing he might say to his nephew, but still. . . ."

"No, I mean where, like in, what park?"

"Scottsdale Stadium. Arizona. Which was strangely appropriate, because. . . ."

"Oh. Thin air."

Thin air. I may have to get another T-shirt that says "I HIT A BASEBALL 350 FEET AND WHY IS IT THAT EVERYONE'S

REACTION IS 'THIN AIR'?" The whole trouble with my baseball career, and my life, is that my T-shirts have to have too many words on them.

My game shirt, the authentic Chicago away uniform shirt I was wearing when I hit the ball 350 feet, has only one word on it: "CUBS." The All-Star Baseball School's weeklong camp last month for men over thirty-five, which culminated with a game against some of the '69 Cubs, was the closest I will come to fitting myself into that word, that one round patch.

How close was that?

What? Who are you with?

This was an oft fantasized experience you had, right? So this is your oft fantasized interview.

About time.

You weren't satisfied with your press coverage at the camp?

No. *Time* magazine unaccountably attributed my 350-foot shot to Art Lessel, a sixty-three-year-old pilot.

Yeah, but what about the thin air?

I'll tell you about thin air. Thin air is when Randy Hundley, who was one of the former Cubs I played against, pops a ball incalculably high into what we call the Big Arizona Sky. Being camped under a fly in Arizona is like looking over the side of a boat after a camera you just dropped into Lake Michigan. And I'll tell you something else about thin air. Thin air is when I, the third baseman, fresh from the triumph of hitting a ball 350 feet, find myself in the position of having to come to grips with a pop-up that resembles the average person's concept of a pop-up about as much as Ralph Sampson resembles your gym teacher.

In other words, a tough chance.

But that's not all. To try to catch it, I have to drift toward the same spot where, in 1970, I had my darkest day as a sportswriter, when Leo Durocher — who managed the Cubs then and was managing them again in this game — branded me as the anti-Cub right there in front of the whole team. Anyway, I miss it.

Really? The pop-up? Why do you miss it?

I don't miss it now. I missed it then. And three days later it's on national TV. At least my friends and I think that's me we see, though I find out much later it's some other guy missing a different pop-up. But by then, the damage to my psyche and reputation had been done.

What were you called? You and the other sixty-two men over thirty-five who, for $2,195 each, lived out a boyhood dream by working out with major leaguers?

"Campers." I would have liked "prospects" better. By the way, two or three guys under thirty-five slipped in. Can you imagine how far I would have hit the ball if I'd been their age? I'm forty-one! True, I never hit a ball that far when I *was* under thirty-five. That was the longest ball I ever hit in my life. And maybe the last. What a way to go out! But what if I'm getting better? What if I have yet to come into my oft fantasized-own? Baseball! You just won't let go! I might say, however, that it was never my boyhood dream to miss a pop-up in front of thousands of people.

The All-Star School, which is operated by Hundley and Chicago entrepreneur Allan Goldin, usually instructs kids, right?

Yes, we were the historic first middle-aged campers. And we seem to have struck a chord. Every television network was all over us. Another Cub camp, also in Scottsdale, is planned for April, and a company called Baseball Fantasies Fulfilled has announced an April camp in Tempe featuring old Dodgers.

How did the Cub camp work?

Very well. We had the Scottsdale facilities that the Cubs formerly used for spring training, and we were drilled in fundamentals by '69 Cubs Hundley, Jenkins, Billy Williams, Ron Santo, Ernie Banks, Glenn Beckert, Jim Hickman, Rich Nye, Ken Rudolph and Gene Oliver, and by slightly later-vintage Cubs Jose Cardenal and Steve Stone. The old Cubs also played with us in intrasquad games. Nobody wanted to look like a jerk in front of them. Take away the Cubs and the camp would have degenerated into middle-aged doctors, lawyers, brokers, and businessmen rolling around on the ground fighting over whose bat it was. There should be Cubs at the U.N.

And on the last day of camp, in Scottsdale Stadium — where the fences are all deeper than 350 feet — before around 4,200 fans and a host of media folks who don't really care about the longest ball a person ever hit in his entire life, the Old Cubs beat us 23–6.

Does that mean you were seventeen runs short of being as good as a team of major leaguers, one of whom, Jenkins, is still active, and, incidentally, is 6 feet 5 inches and is the guy who caught your soaring drive over his shoulder?

It's hard to say. I do know that I came within about 15 inches of catching what you would call a major-league pop-up. I remember thinking to myself, while drifting over toward the spot in foul territory where I first met Durocher in 1970, "Oh, well, God, I guess . . . mine." Privately, I hoped that Jimmy Stuart, a commodities trader in Chicago who won the plaque for Most Aggressive Camper, would hustle pushily over from shortstop and call me off of it, and I would've given him a look of annoyance and let him have it. But he didn't.

I looked up at that thing. And what struck me was, "This pop-up doesn't care who I am." Also, the sun was in my eyes. "The sun is in my eyes," I thought. "And I *still* don't know what made Durocher say what he said in 1970. And anyway, what in the hell am I supposed to do with this thing? I'm a writer. I'm forty-one years old. And I was never all that good when I was twenty-one. And it's not even really spring yet. The pop-ups are ahead of the third basemen. And . . ."

And you missed it . . . Could you give us an idea of what a typical day in camp was like?

Thank you for changing the subject. First of all, we take a bus from our hotel to the '69 Cubs' spring workout fields (now used by the Giants) on Hayden Road, where we enter a dressing room and don big-league uniforms. Right? Most of us would have been willing to die at that point. All right, my pants were too big. But if angels offered me a golden robe,

would I say, "only if you've got it in a 44 long"? And the old
Cubs are sitting around telling stories about Durocher, their
manager in '69 (as well as '70, when I met him), and how hard
he was on nonregulars, whom he referred to as "the rest of
you bleep." There was the time Lee Thomas went up to
pinch-hit and Durocher sat on the bench saying, "Look at that
bleep bleep bleep. He can't run, he can't hit, I don't know
why the bleep bleep bleep I got him. Look at him! He's going
to pop up." And sure enough, Thomas popped up. Durocher
swore for several minutes, then turned to Ted Savage and
told him to pinch-hit next. "Why should I go up there," said
Savage, "and subject myself to abuse?"

*Would you say you were subjected to big-league baseball with-
out the abuse?*

Well, to some extent. In all candor, I would have to say
that this was where the $2,195 came in. Half of that may have
been for overhead and the other half for not having Durocher
come in until the end of the week. But there was some abuse,
after all. There were all those reporters. And aerobics.

Aerobics were led by Susie Warren, who is what you might
call lithe. And she made us campers do terrible things with
our bodies, to music. Cardenal would accompany us, using a
bat as a baton and crying *"No mas! No mas!"* Otherwise, the
Cubs grunted and groaned with the rest of us. I have found it
possible to live a normal life without reflecting upon the fact
that I have hamstrings. I did not find this possible while
performing aerobics.

Hamstrings a-twang, we would leave Susie and take on the
easier part of the day: playing hardball. We would divide into
five squads and rotate from field to field and Cub to Cub.
Williams showed me that I'd been holding a bat wrong all my
life. You're supposed to hold it up in the forward, or fingers,
part of the hand, not back up against the pad. Because
when — or if — you hit a ball thrown at big-league batting-
practice speed with the bat held back up against your pad,
your right pad, if you bat right-handed, turns various shades
of blue. This subject arose when I asked Williams why I had
developed indigo hand.

It·was Santo who explained why I'd developed it on my left hand, too. That was because I've been holding the glove wrong all my life. You're supposed to hold it so that the ball always hits in the webbing, he said. This was a piece of advice I was unable to use. I feel I'm doing well when I catch a ball with any part of the leather. Playing third base, I also developed indigo shoulder, chest, and thigh.

Hickman and Jenkins also explained to me that I'd been holding the ball wrong all my life. If you hold it along the seams, it veers. This is what Jenkins usually does, because as a pitcher he usually wants it to veer. This is what Hickman never did, because as a fielder he didn't want it to. This is what I, as a fielder, have often done down through the veers.

There are a great many intangibles in baseball, aren't there?

Yes, and I wonder whether I will ever get a feel for them.

What else would you do on a typical day of training, after finding out that you've always been holding everything wrong?

Go back to the dressing room. Sit around sweaty. Take a shower with a member of the Hall of Fame, Banks, who's saying, "There is a vast reservoir of potential in all of us waiting to be tapped!" Stiffen up. Walk out toward the bus like somebody who just got off a horse. Yet feel *primed*. Feel *bodily*.

And go back to the hotel and sit in the whirlpool with the Cubs. Santo tells about the time Rogers Hornsby went through the Cubs' minor-league camps checking out all the hitters. Hornsby called a bunch of them together in some bleachers and went down the rows. The first guy was black. "You better go back to shining shoes," Hornsby said, "because you can't hit." And he said more or less the same thing to one prospect after another. Santo and Williams were sitting together. "If he says that to me," Santo said to Williams, "I'm going to cry." And Hornsby came to Williams. "You," Hornsby said, "can hit in the big leagues right now." And he said the same thing to Santo.

Later, Santo was up in the bigs, in the All-Star Game. "And there are McCovey and Aaron and Mays, and Ron Santo, and some photographer is taking a picture of us together!" Santo says, beaming. We beam with him. Not only campers but also Cubs are returned to their youth.

Would you say that rejuvenation was a theme of the camp?

Yes. But also fading. The '69 Cubs, you know, were the team that blew the National League East title to the Miracle Mets. The Cubs looked as if they were going to run away with it. Until September. On the first day of camp, Hundley gave Stone, who was to be our coach in the big Friday game against the Cubs, a chance to address us. "Just stay close to them till Thursday," Stone advised. "These are the '69 Cubs. They fade."

I asked Banks how he knew when it was time to retire. "You lose your quickness," he said. "And you hear whispers. Rumors. 'He used to make that play.' 'He used to hit that pitch.' Or maybe they don't say anything, but you can see it when they look at you. You can see it in their eyes."

That sounded like what I had been going through since I was twelve. In my last Little League season I was pretty good, but since then it has been only flashes. Moments. Inklings of what it feels like to be a player.

Did you have any of those inklings with the Cubs?

I had so many inklings, I may never sort them out. "You look like you've played some ball," Hundley told me, and to give you some idea how that made me feel, here's a story. A reporter at the camp overheard some of the Cubs saying that Ken Schwab, a fifty-five-year-old Illinois grain-farmer owner, looked pretty good. After asking another camper to point out Schwab, the reporter went up to another person he thought had been indicated and said, "Hey, the Cubs are saying you look pretty good." The guy nearly fainted. "My lifelong dream!" he cried. "You can't imagine what this means to me. For a big-league player to say, 'Irvin Singletary looks pretty good!'" (I have changed his name.) Here's how I felt: 1) "I *have* played some ball! I have played some ball. I must have! All those years, some of the time, anyway, that was actually *ball* I was playing!" And 2) "*Me?*"

Then, too, there were simpler moments. Grounder hit at

me, bing-bing-tapocketta, it's in my glove, I'm up with it smoothly, throwing, zip, it's over to the first baseman chest high, a couple of murmurs among the campers: "Got an arm."

"Don't throw too hard too soon," Santo tells me. And the next day he asks me, "How's your hose?"

It wouldn't have sounded much sweeter if it had been Jessica Lange asking.

How was your hose?

My hose was there, all right. My hose wasn't dead.

You sound surprised.

The irony of all this is that before the opportunity to play with the Cubs arose, I had planned to retire from organized ball. I had given Willie Stargell, who is my age, the chance to hang it up first. I didn't want to steal any of his thunder. This spring I was going to make a simple announcement.

There had been certain telltale signs. For instance, when the slo-pitch softball team that you think you belong to fails to inform you that the season is under way, you begin to wonder. That happened two seasons ago. Then, too, I had doubts about my hose.

The one thing I've had in baseball was an arm from third base. Aside from a tendency to hit, at best, singles to right and on defense to stare off into space, I've been, since Little League, a classic third baseman: too slow to run or to hide. And when the ball bounced off some part of my body, I could pick it up and make that throw. If my hose wasn't out of sorts.

Also, I could never hit slo-pitch softball pitching, which was the only kind I seemed likely to face again. I don't like a pitch that goes way up in the air. When I go to bed at night and either pitch or bat myself to sleep, I see curves, sliders, screwballs, and hummers. I can't hit pitching that I never see in my dreams.

You were going to confine yourself to fandom, then?

No, I thought I might go on as a sort of pitcher in the rye. Throwing batting practice to the young. You groove the ball to somebody, and he or she hits it on the nose and you both feel good. And so do people watching. It's like a comedy act.

And it's interesting, because you can fail at it. In Scottsdale I threw BP to Santo, and I pressed too hard and didn't get the ball where he or I wanted it, and he kept popping it up. I got the feeling he was pressing, too, trying to hit pitches he should've laid off so I wouldn't feel bad. I pressed harder. It was like strained conversation. I wonder whether something like that wasn't going on between the '69 Cubs in the stretch, when they let each other down.

Do you have much experience throwing batting practice?

Ah. At the highest level of serious competition I reached, high school, that was my forte. Somebody once told me he'd run into my old high school coach, Ray Thurmond, who remembered me as a pitcher. I was, of course, a third baseman, but it was at throwing batting practice that I shone. I wore a hole in my right high-school baseball shoe throwing BP without a pitcher's toe. Those are the spikes I wore against the Cubs.

The shoes of a congenial player, a giving player.

Many people might prefer that their old coach remember them the way Durocher remembers Eddie Stanky, as one of those "scratching, hungry, diving ballplayers who come to kill you."

That's the kind of player I wanted to be. Scrappy. I remember the only time I ever broke up a double play. I was playing intramural softball, in college. Hit the second baseman just right, flipped him up into the air. Didn't hurt him, though. I actually think he enjoyed it, too. This is a terrible thing for someone who pretends to understand serious ball to say, but my deepest desire in sports isn't to win but to share a good time. Maybe that's why Durocher seemed outraged at the very sight of me, that day in 1970.

This was the incident that occurred over in foul territory near the third-base dugout, where you missed the pop-up?

I wish you wouldn't keep harping on that pop-up. To me, if I *catch* a pop-up that goes as high as the Washington Monument, that's news. Or if I hit a ball 350 feet. But to my critics and friends, the idea of me camped not quite under a pop-up, and tilting slightly to the left, and tilting slightly farther to the

left, and then the ball coming down well beyond my grasp —
that's their idea of something worthy of comment. What
people usually say to me now, if I'm unable to start the
conversation off on the right note, is, "I hear that you missed
a pop-up."

*I'm sorry. There are so many other things I wanted to ask
you. Like, how did you prepare for the Cubs?*

For the first time in my life, I worked out. I hate to work
out. You have an angel on one shoulder saying "Go, go, go"
and a devil on the other saying "Stop, stop, stop," and there
you are in between, bored to death with the whole argument
and wallowing in sheer, but not pleasant, kinesthesia.

I like to play ball. A ball takes you out of yourself. Of
course, if you miss a ball, you snap back into yourself pretty
quick, but then you have a lot to talk over with yourself. Even
while you are out of yourself, you can be narrating semicon-
sciously. "He can still hit," you can be saying, referring to
yourself in the third person. "Ball was in on him but he got
that bat head out in front." The main reason I cover sports is
so I can keep the vocabulary of my semiconscious narration
up-to-date.

Now looming ahead of me was a shot at living that narration. I was there to write about it, sure, but it meant a lot
more to me than that. So, do you know what I did? I lifted
weights. Not only do I not like lifting weights, I deplore it.
However, a person doesn't get many chances later on in life
to whang a well-pitched baseball or to snag a well-hit one. A
person doesn't want to come back from such a change to
report to his family, "I was overpowered."

My son has 10-pound dumbbells lying around the house. I
started pumping them and swinging them and going through
throwing and batting motions with them, and I didn't stop
even when my daughter would collapse — her preroga-
tive — in helpless laughter. I also split two cords of firewood
down to the biggest pile of kindling in Massachusetts.

*When you first encountered the wily hardball in Arizona,
how did you feel?*

Overpowered.

A hardball is a thing that, when you have not seen one with steam on it in many years, is upon you before you know it. And in the field I was lost in the complexity of hops. Grounders were like logarithms. Also, I didn't seem to hinge in the same places I used to. And my throwing was so zipless the first day that it moved me to compose a blues song:

> I used to have a rifle,
> I used to have a gun.
> Lord, Lord.
> I used to have a rifle,
> I used to have a gun.
> Now that ball floats over
> Like a cinnamon bun.

But you said your hose wasn't dead.

Several things happened. One is that our trainer, Harry Jordan, manipulated my arm and discovered that the tendon over the funny bone had popped out. At least that's what he claimed. He popped it back in. I've never heard of anyone being plagued by funny-bone-tendon problems before, but I know that as he worked, Harry made terrific deep crunching noises in his throat that served to keep some of the faint-hearted campers out of the training room altogether, so I'm willing to believe that Jordan was a funnybonologist.

Another thing that kept me going early in camp was my chewing. I was chewing good. I talked chewing on a knowledgeable basis with Jenkins, who bites right into an open can of snuff with his lower front teeth. I could chew with the big boys. I even chewed during aerobics. This helped.

Also, nobody was yelling at anybody. The spirit of Durocher wasn't in the camp. I don't respond to being yelled at. It distracts me from yelling at myself.

Then, too, I had all of my clichés working.

I thought sportswriters are supposed to eschew clichés.

Sportswriters, yes. Ballplayers use them to hone their concentration.

I was being interviewed by a TV crew. Most campers were

interviewed so many times that they eventually stopped calling their wives to tell them to turn on the VCR.

"Are you feeling the pressure?" I was asked.

"Nah," I lied. "When the bell rings, the juices will flow."

And I spat. Television likes visual touches. If you want to get a statement heard and seen all across the land, remember to spit right after making it.

Then, all of a sudden, I picked up a ball the way the first caveman picked up the first good fist-sized rock. And I felt my hose start to fill with water again. I felt leaner, stronger, springier, *glad* to have hamstrings. The downside of this was that my pants became even baggier. But I wore a psychic T-shirt that said "PLAYING MYSELF INTO SHAPE."

And then you went on a tear, right?

No. Then I reached my nadir. I thought I had reached my nadir years ago, several times, but in the very first intrasquad game I hit another new low.

Because I let the guys down. "We are here," Banks had announced one day behind the batting cage, "to ameliorate the classic polarization of the self-motivated individual and the ideology of the group."

Excuse me. Did Banks say things like that often?

Banks said things that came from the Big Arizona Sky. When someone asked him whether he felt he had come along too soon, before the days of astronomical baseball salaries, he said, "No. Wish I'd been born sooner. With the philosophers. Days of Plato, and Socrates, and Alexander Graham Bell." When I asked him what would be a thrill for him comparable to the thrill we campers were getting, he said, "To sing in the Metropolitan Opera."

What Banks most often said was, "*Veez*-ualize yourself hitting a home run!"

"Ernie," said a camper, "I thought we were just supposed to meet the ball, and it would take care of itself."

"No," he said. "It won't. It will not take care of itself. You have to see yourself inside the ball when it is in the pitcher's hand, and you're thinking, 'Time to take a long ride.'"

But don't change the subject. I'm ready to discuss my nadir.

You have a lot of heart as an interviewee, you know that?

Yes, but in the first intrasquad game, I made several plays of the kind that kill infield chatter. Here I was feeling, "Give me Jimmy Stuart and Bob Margolin and Bill Mitchell and Dennis Albano and Wally Pecs (best ballplayer's name in camp) and Dennis Ferrazzano and Tim Tyers and Scott Mermel and George Altemose and Dave Schultz and Steve Heiferman and the Arnold, Crawford, and Patti brothers, and I could take on anybody in the world." And what do I do in the first intrasquad game? I drop a line drive hit right at me. A third baseman who can't catch a line drive at his sternum is as dependable as a frog that can't balance on a lily pad. And I let an easy grounder go under my glove. That's like letting a baby's head bob around. And Margolin, who in real life runs a vanity press but is no one's vanity catcher, whips a throw down to nip a guy stealing third, but I don't dig it out of the dirt. In Arizona a lot of thin air can get between a person and the ball — and between a person and his mates, even if they don't yell at you.

And the first time at bat, I dribble into a double play. The next time, Stone is pitching. "Can you hit a curveball?" he asks me.

"No," I say.

He throws me a curveball.

And you miss it?

No. Worse. I take it on the inside corner. And this is what I hear, from Oliver on the other bench: "That's a hanger, Roy." I've just taken a hanging curveball for a strike! What Stone has done is throw me a curve that I could hit. And I took it! That's like Jack Benny giving you a straight line and you saying, "Oh. Excuse me. I wasn't listening."

Like I say, nobody yelled at us campers, but every now and then one of the big-leaguers would give us a quiet, chastening line, like, "Got to have that one," or, "That's where we need you, big man." The social fabric. The ideology of the group.

The next pitch from Stone isn't a hanger. Not a curve. It's down the pipe. And I go after it. "All right!" I think.

The ball intersects with my bat about three inches from my hands. It pops weakly to the catcher. I feel as if I've reached out for a proffered ice-cream cone and found it in my armpit. "Well," I think, "I am losing my mind."

That was your nadir?

Yes. It didn't help that I had margarita tongue from the night before.

Ah, I've always wondered about the big-league night life. What did you do that night?

For one thing, talked to Cardenal about creekus.

What are creekus?

"You know, creekus," Cardenal said. "Little things." He made sawing motions with his arms like a cricket producing sounds. "One time in Chicago I come to the park with my eyes swollen shut. 'Cause I couldn't sleep. 'Cause creekus was in my room all night. So I can't play. And Mike Royko in the paper, ohhh, he got on me.

"And last night in my room? Creekus again. I find seven of them behind the toilet. I kill them all. I go back to bed. I hear more creekus. I turn the light back on. I find five creekus behind the television. I call the desk. 'You got to send the exterminator!' If Royko had been there! I could have shown him creekus!"

But, you came back from that nadir, right?

Let me put it this way. The next evening I'm in the coffee shop. I eat a well-earned sandwich. I sign the check. And there's a place on the check for "comments." So I write, "I went three-for-five today." There not being much room, I didn't bother to add, "and fielded flawlessly."

What turned you around?

After my nadir, I talked to Stone. He told me about his Cy Young season with Baltimore in 1980, after which he had nothing left. "I threw over 60 percent breaking balls," he said. "I knew it would ruin my arm, but I was winning fifteen games in a row. One year of twenty-five and seven is worth five of fifteen and fifteen." Before a game, he said, he would take a Percodan if he felt he would need it in addition to the four aspirin he would routinely take every three innings. And he kept breaking off those hooks.

"Well," I sighed, "your straight one was too tough for me."

"No, that was my forkball," he said.

"Oh!" I said. My heart leapt. "What does it do?"

"Drops off like a spitball and moves in on you. Nobody can hit it."

No wonder you didn't hit it.

Precisely. Not only that, but I'd had a real major-league experience. I'd popped up a forkball. The next day, when we played our next intrasquad game, I was ready.

Would you like to tell us about it?

Single to right off Dr. Harry Soloway, the Chicago shrink who became nationally famous by telling the *Today* show that he wasn't giving any more interviews because the last reporter he talked to called him "the most inept ballplayer I have ever seen, man or boy." Except for his fame, a single to right off Dr. Harry Soloway is not an enduring achievement, but a solid single is a solid single. Then, off Cardenal, I ground out and single up the middle. Then, off Beckert, I fly left. I'm pulling the ball!

A portent. For the 350. . . .

Although I don't realize it at the time. But now we get down to the last inning. Bases loaded. Beckert, who has been moving painfully and saying, "Now I remember why I retired," wants to get the game over. He's working in and out on me. This feels like actual baseball! Three and two. Comes in with a high, tight fastball. Too close to take. I foul it back. This is probably a thrill for Beckert, too: a second baseman getting a chance to work on a hitter. He delivers a funny-looking pitch on the outside corner.

And what do you do with it?

Rip it. On a line. But not a straight line. More satisfying than that. A line like a scimitar blade. Over the first baseman's head, and it *bites* the ground three feet fair. It goes blisteringly on its way, and I say to it, "Burn!"

A double. And such a double! I am most of the way to third when I see the runner ahead of me running toward me. Fortunately, he's heading back toward third, not second. He has become conservative and decided he can't score. But this is such a double that I am able to turn around and go 70 feet back into second standing up. I have hit the equivalent of a triple and a half.

That must have been a thrill.

I'll tell you the thrill. The thrill is what Beckert exclaims.

What does Beckert exclaim?

Beckert exclaims, "How did you hit that pitch?" He turns to Jenkins, who's umpiring. "Slider right on the outside corner!" he says. "And I had him set up!"

"I was looking for it," I reply.

"That's right!" says Jenkins. "That's a good hitter."

Wow! You were looking for it?

No. I lied. The truth was I had found my strength as a hitter. Which turned out to be very similar to my strength as a defensive back in football — which is that I am too slow to take a fake. My strength as a hitter, I now realize, is that I haven't got sense enough to be set up. Why do you think a person becomes a writer? It's because he can never figure anything out until afterward. In baseball down through the years I've often been trying, during the seventh inning, to figure out what happened in the fifth. And what happened was that I wasn't paying attention because I was wondering what I did wrong in the third. And what I did wrong in the third was boot one because I was thinking, "I've got to concentrate with every fiber of my being. Hmm, interesting phrase. I wonder what all the fibers of my being in concert would look like? A nice wool shirt?" Oh, those rare great moments in sports when my mind isn't working and my body is!

Another thing I do in this game is throw four guys out with my hose. My mind is a blank then, too.

Did you talk your triple and a half over with Beckert and Jenkins later?

No, not exactly. But I will say this. In my time I'd

exchanged various glances with ballplayers. And a major-league manager once mistook me for a member of the Hall of Fame. That was when I called Billy Martin on the phone, and hearing my voice, he cried, "Mick? Mick? Is it the Mick?" He thought I was Mickey Mantle. When he realized I wasn't we were both very disappointed.

But I had never exchanged a glance with a ballplayer that contained any hint that I, too, was a part of the actual ballplaying experience. One time, a Venezuelan sportscaster, Juan Vené, and I told Manny Sanguillen, when he was catching for the Pirates, that we had played baseball on opposing press teams.

"Softball?" asked Sanguillen.

"No, hardball."

Sanguillen was one of the most gracious ballplayers I've ever met. But Sanguillen shook his head and said, "You guys!"

That evening in Scottsdale after the second intrasquad game, I exchanged glances with Beckert and Jenkins that, to me — and I am talking in terms of diamond experience now — contained a hint of "us guys."

Tell me. This is another thing I have always wondered about. Do you ballplayers put your pants on one leg at a time, like everybody else?

I can only speak for myself. The answer in my case is: not always. After that intrasquad game, I got tired putting one leg on, stopped for a while and worked on the other one.

But you were ready for the big game the next day in Scottsdale Stadium?

Did I tell you I hit a ball 350 feet?

In passing, but tell me more about it.

I have always gotten on well with veterinarians. Rich Nye, who won twenty-six games in the big leagues, is now a veterinarian. If I didn't live so far from Des Plaines, Illinois, I'd send my dogs to him. Nye threw me a good pitch to hit.

Every camper got one at bat in the big game. By the time I got up, in the ninth or tenth of many innings, it had become clear that a few winded old Cubs are better than wave after fresh wave of old brokers, law professors, and salesmen. The crowd was diminished and restive.

"Representing *Sports Illustrated*," blared the loudspeaker, "Ray" and a mispronunciation of my last name. I strode to the plate and realized I didn't have on a helmet. I ran back and got one. I strode to the plate and realized that the flap covered the wrong ear. I ran back and got a left-eared one. Fan reaction indicated a doubting of my expertise. I dug in.

"Coming right down the middle," said Rudolph, who was catching.

All you selfless, unrecognized batting-practice pitchers out there, Keep it up! Your service will be repaid. Someday a veterinarian will lay one in there for you. In practice, Nye had shown me his real 80-mile-per-hour fastball, which I nearly hit. This one was a notch slower. Later he said he wished he'd thrown it harder; I would have cleared the fence. But I'll take my 350 feet, and the sound of a crowd that came to scoff and stayed to eat its heart out.

Anything else you'd like to say?

Yeah. I got my longest hit ever against a team managed by Leo Durocher.

Did I tell you about the first time I met Leo? It was in Scottsdale Stadium in the spring of 1970 that I, a cub reporter, innocently introduced myself to him. And he, standing outside the third-base dugout, pointed his finger at me and began to address, at the top of his lungs, the players who, a few months before, had been the '69 Cubs: "I want everybody to hear this! I'm not talking to this guy! I'm not saying a word!"

Just before he disappeared under the stands, he turned and added, "And he knows why!"

I didn't then and don't now. But it got to me. I loved baseball, and Durocher went all the way back through Willie Mays and Coogan's Bluff and the Gashouse Gang to Ruth. I couldn't shake the feeling that there must be something about me that didn't fit into the national pastime.

Did you ever run into Durocher again?

ROY ALTON BLOUNT JR.
Name pronounced Blunt.

Born Oct. 4, 1941, at Indianapolis, Ind.
Height, depends. Weight, depends.
Throws and bats righthanded.
Hobby — Raising mixed-breed dogs.
Attended Vanderbilt University, Nashville, Tenn., and Harvard
    University, Cambridge, Mass.

Year	Club	League	Pos.	B.A.
1951	Tigers†	Little	OF	.063
1952	Tigers	Little	OF	.179
1953	Tigers	Little	3B	.320
1954	* (Did not play)			
1955	Pels	Babe Ruth	3B	.213
1956	Pels	Babe Ruth	3B	.265
1956	Decatur High B-Team	Region 4-AA	3B	.213
1957	Decatur High B-Team	Region 4-AAA	3B	.270
1958	Decatur High Varsity§	Region 4-AAA	3B	.000
1959	Decatur High Varsity x	Region 4-AAA	3B-1B	.000
1960–70	* (Did not play)			
1971	Sports Illustrated vs. NY Press in Yankee Stadium, one game		C	.500
1972	NY Press vs. Venezuelan Press in Venezuela, three games y		3B	.400
1973	NY Press vs. Venezuelan Press in Yankee Stadium, one game z		2B	.500
1974	* (Did not play)			
1983	All-Star Campers vs. each other and '69 Cubs, three games a		3B	.375
Totals	(In major league stadium or uniform)			.409
	(Not in major league stadium or uniform)			.201

† Nearly everyone else was bigger.
* On temporary inactive list.
§ Not very many at bats.
x Hardly any at bats.
y Wore New York Yankee and Met uniforms.
z Wore Yankee uniform.
a Wore Chicago Cub uniform. (Got to keep it. For $80.)

Not until camp week thirteen years later. At the banquet after the big game, he took the occasion to make an emotional talk. He confessed why the '69 Cubs folded: "They didn't give me 100 percent."

What a thing to say at this point! Would the man never let up?

"They gave me 140 percent." Ah. The Cubs had pressed. Durocher was conceding that he'd chewed on them too hard.

He also apologized publicly for embarrassing Santo nastily in a celebrated 1971 clubhouse meeting. After the banquet, Durocher and Santo embraced.

Durocher didn't apologize to me. He glared at me once but with no hint of recognition. He had relieved me, however, of one burden. I still don't know what made me anathema, but I do know it wasn't my fault that the Cubs didn't win in '69.

"Winning the pennant that year might have been anticlimactic for the kind of love we had on that team," said emcee Gene Oliver from the podium. However that may be, in 1969 Durocher seems, oddly enough, to have forged a team that couldn't win but did learn how to share a good time.

So you have no complaints?

No complaints? No complaints? What madman built a stadium whose fences are nowhere shorter than 355 feet?

Let me quote to you the testimony of Steve Stone, and also of longtime Chicago baseball writer Richard Dozer, now of *The Phoenix Gazette,* who was as much of an official scorer as we had: "The ball is out in Fenway."

But . . . the air in Fenway isn't thin.

Yeah, and Hundley's pop-up doesn't go nearly so high, and I catch it and toss it over to Leo.

Bernie Lincicome

The Long-Suffering
Now Insufferable

Chicago Tribune, September 30, 1984

It is not possible, we are being told, to be a true Cub fan unless you can remember curb feelers, pin boys and the Andrews Sisters who, of course, once played in the Wrigley outfield as Patty, Laverne and Bubba.

You have no right to appreciate the 1984 Cubs unless you laughed at the 1954 Cubs, or took one home to dinner.

It is necessary to be at least pre-Bull, better to be pre-Ernie and best to be pre-ivy to be an authentic Cub fan, though the worthiest Cub fans are only those who are pre-fire.

I imagine the year the Cubs won their first modern-era pennant, back in 1906, one old-timer sniffing over his beer at the kid in the new straw hat, "World Series? That ain't nuthin'. You ought to been around here when no one knowed the game from stoop tag. Sissies. These new guys is sissies, wearin' hand gloves to catch the ball. You can't even hit 'em with the ball when they run no more. Next thing you know they'll be wearin' numbers on their shirts when a real fan can tell a Cub just by the hang of his mustache."

Cub fandom is apparently a very precious thing, to be jealously guarded and not to be passed around to strangers, who can be defined as anyone not named, including middle initial, in the original Burnham Plan, the Mayflower Compact of Chicago.

If your name is not on the list, you must be able to prove that neither you nor any of your ancestors ever drank imported beer or lived in any building with more than three floors. Suburbs don't count.

Suburbs, in fact, count double points against you. Anyone with a lawn is a fraud. And anyone with a riding mower is not worth the energy it takes to kick-start one.

The pedigree of a Cub fan can be measured by the number of "L" stops he lives away from Wrigley Field, unless he has moved in some time after Leo Durocher moved out or if he plays racquetball.

A real Cub fan sits only in the bleachers, without a shirt, which, when worn, has neither a reptile on the pocket nor a tie around the neck, though it may have pizza down the front since real Cub fans know that Chicago pizza makes a terrific seat cushion.

There are three classes of Cub fans — real Cub fans, new Cub fans and TV Cub fans, the last being roundly resented because not only are they recent and remote but are wired for cable.

Cub fans who have moved away from the Loop, to places with two names, the first one being San or the last one being Beach, no longer qualify for Cub fandom. They have forfeited whatever claim to the Cubs they might have earned in their youth. If they were real Cub fans, they would have remained and suffered like everyone else. The real Cub fan sees these exiles as no better than peacetime soldiers trying to join the VFW.

The most condemned· of all are the recent arrivals to Cubdom, even though many of them are the Cubs themselves, and one of which am I. We are the least entitled of anyone to share in the community warmth brought on by the success of the 1984 Cubs.

We are told we have not earned the right of comparison, having no disappointment against which to measure the recent relief. How, we are asked, can you appreciate a full stomach if it has never been empty?

Simple envy, that's what it is.

It is as if we've come in at the end of a bad mystery and are able to tell who dunnit without even knowing who the suspects were.

We have the happy advantage of being able to measure all future Cubs teams from this one, like having a fresh sheet of paper with only one name on it. Easier to carry, too.

I don't apologize for catching the passing bandwagon. All I had to do was stick out my arm.

Not only have I never witnessed a losing Cub season, I am innocent enough to believe that this is the way it is supposed to be.

I am foolish enough to imagine that failure should not be deeded from season to season, that there doesn't have to be penance before pleasure, and that I can admire the accomplishments of this Cubs team even if I can't tell you which side of the plate George Altman used to strike out from.

I have the same amount of regret for missing all the frustration of the last 39 years as I had for getting a vaccination to avoid smallpox.

What are bandwagons for, if not to jump on?

Lonnie Wheeler

Opening Day, April 1987

Bleachers: A Summer in Wrigley Field

I'd always thought of Wrigley Field's bleachers as the place where real baseball fans go when they close their eyes and click their heels three times. On television, I'd seen all those home runs disappearing into the thick crowd in the cheap seats in left field, and I imagined those same happily suffering souls, shorn of their shirts and pretenses, sticking it out together through all the bittersweet seasons.

I had been to the bleachers only once in my life, on a crowded Saturday with my wife. I didn't know what they were like on weekdays or hot days or windy days or most days, and yet I knew, as baseball fans instinctively seem to know, that the bleacher seat at Wrigley Field was the best place in the world to watch a ballgame. I thought of the bleachers as a window on baseball, and the view as pure as if the glass had been broken out on a foul ball by the kid next door. I thought of them as the balcony over baseball's summertime serenade. I was going to spend the season there, and I thought it would be baseball heaven.

On Opening Day 1987, it was apparent that I had underestimated the place. To the 3,260 people packed into them — plus standing room — the bleachers were much more than benches beyond the outfield. They were a neighborhood, a bar, a depot, a beach, an office, a church, a home. They were a ward of Chicago, and I stood against the fence behind the

four-dollar seats in left field on Opening Day and felt like a
stranger. It was strange being a stranger in a ballpark, sort of
like being at a party where everybody figures you must know
somebody they know. People hugged each other, friends
lost over the grim Chicago winter and found again with the
first pitch. They shook hands with the beer vendors. Two
women I had never seen before, stockbrokers named Mimi
and Kate, asked if I wanted something from the concession
stand.

It was Yankee Doodle Tuesday in Chicago, Opening Day
and Election Day all wrapped up in an apple-pie April seventh.
No other place observes both baseball and politics with the
same fervency as Chicago — it is equally judgmental of its
aldermen and its outfielders — and to a stranger, the afternoon seemed as privately provincial as it was classically
American. Outside the ballpark, a large black man walked in
front of an important-looking procession, and I reasoned that
he must be the incumbent mayor, Harold Washington, with
his entourage. I asked the guy standing next to me about it.
He looked at me like I had underwear on my head and said,
"Vrdolyak." I explained that I had taken the large black man
for Washington, and the guy said, "That was probably the
bodyguard. Are you from another planet?" It seemed that I
was. Place called Ohio.

The bleachers were a world that a visitor could admire for
its sights and society, but he would have to live with the
natives for a while before he could understand them. More
and more, ballparks were ballparks, and being in one was
like being in another shopping mall with five shoe stores, a
chocolate-chip cookie shop, and patient husbands sitting around
the fountain. But the bleachers were *somewhere*. They were
a place settled and developed by a city and a sport, indigenous
turf, a tract of Americana whose essential nature could not be
contained by the brick walls of Wrigley Field, or the streets
named Clark, Addison, Waveland, and Sheffield. In a way, the
bleachers were bigger than the ballpark. They were an icon,
a culture, a Windy City fingerprint. They were an open floor

on which a big town danced its parochial polka. And the music started on April seventh.

For the charming if somewhat curious branch of mankind known as Cub fans, spring is a sanguine time of the year. Every spring holds the blithe hope that perhaps this is the season in which Satan will grow weary and ease up on the headlock in which he has diabolically held Chicago's mightily struggling National League baseball team since its last world championship in 1908.

The phenomenal aspect of the Chicago Cubs — the thing that makes them different from any other professional sports franchise in the Americas (other than the fact that they have gone longer than any other without a championship, the closest being the crosstown White Sox, who won the World Series in 1917, and then the Boston Red Sox, who beat the Cubs in 1918) — is that, despite their colossal legacy of losing, the scope and fidelity of their constituency is un-matched and unmitigated. There is no census taken on such a thing, but for whatever reasons — cable television, Wrigley Field, day games, cuteness, whatever — it is eminently probable that the Cubs have more and better fans than any other team in the Western Hemisphere, if not beyond. More people watch them on TV than any other team. It's the Cubs that merchants and farmers talk about around the coffee tables in Tennessee and Nebraska. Early in 1984, before the Cubs caught the country's imagination with their joyous rush to the division title, a newspaper in the major-league wilder-ness of Casper, Wyoming — a place where Chicago's WGN superstation was not available to cable subscribers — con-ducted a readership survey to determine the most popular baseball team in the area, and the Cubs outpolled the second-place Yankees by nearly four to one.

There is nothing like it in all of sports. The Red Sox have the same sort of long-suffering history and traditional appeal, but they have won pennants, and the devotion attending them, while heartfelt and powerful, is essentially confined to

New England. The Yankees and Cowboys and Notre Dame have all been winners. Going into 1987, however, only once in the previous fourteen seasons had the Cubs won more games than they had lost. Excepting 1984, incredibly, they had never been closer than five games to the league or division champion since 1945, when they won the pennant. They had contended for first place on rare occasions — their great collapse of 1969 is all too vividly remembered — but nowhere near often enough to interest a less constant congregation. There was no conventional explanation for their massive, madcap popularity. Neither was there any end to it in sight.

In the spring training they had just concluded — after a season in which they finished in fifth place in the National League East, thirty-seven games behind the Mets — the Cubs had drawn more than 106,000 fans to HoHoKam Park in Mesa, Arizona, and broke the all-time preseason attendance record that they had set in 1985. This was despite the fact that a trip to Arizona was not nearly as expedient by car or as economical by airplane from Chicago as most of the Florida camps were to the Eastern major-league cities. It was the traditional wont of Cub fans, however, to schedule their vacations in March or October, depending on their particular form of optimism. There were those who chose to indulge in the winsome wishful thinking and 73.6-degree average high temperatures of Maricopa County's East Valley, and there were those who reserved a week in October on the fat chance that the Cubbies might reverse the wrongs of recent decades and carry the banner of the great American underdog into the World Series. The latter usually ended up at Disney World or somewhere, but there had been nothing to divert the gush of good hope into the sunny, sensible city of Mesa.

It was the Cubs' good fortune, also — either that, or their doing — that Illinois had contributed more than any other state to Maricopa County's population boom in the late seventies and early eighties. The Cubs were practically the home team. After Cub telecasts went out over cable in 1982, announcers Harry Caray and Steve Stone became so popular in greater Phoenix that they opened two restaurants there. By the middle part of the decade, the Cubs' arrival had become a grand event accompanied by a great convergence of blue upon the East Valley — official seventy-dollar Cub satin warm-up jackets in the cool Mesa mornings; Cub shorts and shirts and hats and visors and earrings and pins and buttons in the comfortable Mesa afternoons. Cynics and St. Louisans might find metaphor in this great expression of blue coming from Cub fans, but it is just a color, not a mood. There isn't a baseball fan anywhere who doesn't feel warm late-summer possibilities in the buoyant breeze of spring. With the Superstition Mountains at their backs in the early spring of 1987, the Cubs looked as they had in so many early springs before: like they could be contenders. It would depend on the pitchers and the kids.

It would depend, really, on things about which little could be presumed. A baseball season never really begins; it just sort of emerges out of the accumulated yesterdays, each new team having its genesis in the several before it, and the previous three years had reported ambiguously on the competitive state of the Chicago Cubs. The seminal event in their recent history had been the intoxicating subdivisional championship of 1984, but two years later, the Cubs appeared before the mirror with their clothes wrinkled and their breath reeking, staring at the glass and wondering what happened.

Although the circumstances were certainly extenuating — in 1985, all five of Chicago's starting pitchers had been injured — the fact was that the first-place finish had been followed by a fourth and a fifth. The players had remained essentially the same through it all, the principal exception being that Shawon Dunston had taken over at shortstop for Larry Bowa. Midway through the 1986 season, however, Dallas Green, the powerful president and general manager, had fired manager Jim Frey and replaced him with a quiet, lanky, former weak-hitting shortstop and mildly successful Yankee manager named Gene Michael, known otherwise as

Stick. With that symbolic if arguable change, at least Green had indicated that he recognized a troubling pattern. This was not an easy acknowledgment for the big executive, a man of prodigious ambition and ego who had basked in an air of infallibility after 1984. Having hand-made the Cubs by trading for Ryne Sandberg, Keith Moreland, Gary Matthews, Larry Bowa, Ron Cey, Dennis Eckersley, Steve Trout, Scott Sanderson, Dick Ruthven, Bob Dernier, and Rick Sutcliffe, Green had reason to regard himself as the team's great deliverer. But as the years went on, the humbling, inevitably mortifying process of Cubness was overtaking him and the men he brought to Chicago. The team didn't run, didn't pitch, didn't hit in the clutch. Green's pre-owned ballclub had been a dream machine in 1984's fast ride, but nobody thought to check whether the odometer had been rolled back.

By the time they arrived in Mesa in 1987, the second-hand Cubs were leaking oil, but at least their chrome still had a shine. Several of the stars — Sandberg, Jody Davis, Moreland, Leon Durham, Sutcliffe, reliever Lee Smith — were ostensibly still in their primes. Dunston's was presumed to be arriving anytime, and any of numerous young or unfamiliar players — outfielders Rafael Palmeiro, Chico Walker, Brian Dayett, and Dave Martinez; and pitchers Jamie Moyer, Greg Maddux, and Drew Hall — had the opportunity and apparently the capacity to make a difference. And then there was Andre Dawson.

After a decorated ten-year career as an outfielder with the Montreal Expos, during which Dawson hit twenty or more home runs seven times, won six Gold Gloves, was Rookie of the Year, Player of the Year, the best player in Montreal history, and according to a *New York Times* survey of major leaguers in 1983, the best player in the game, there wasn't another team in the big leagues that showed the least bit of interest in Dawson as a free agent in the early spring of 1987. The Expos themselves had offered two million dollars for two years, but Dawson, whose tender left knee had been at odds with Montreal's artificial playing surface, was intent upon playing in an outfield that earthworms could inhabit. He was also a better hitter in the daytime, had a .346 career average in the natural light of Wrigley Field, and made it clear that he wanted to be in Chicago. Sutcliffe said he'd chip in one hundred thousand dollars of his own salary if the Cubs would sign Dawson. But when Dawson and his agent, Dick Moss, showed up at HoHoKam Park on March third and told Green he could name the price for a new rightfielder, the Cubs folded their arms. Finally, Moss handed Green a blank contract and said that Dawson would sign it that way, with the salary to be determined by the Cubs.

Green still demurred, insisting that no single player could improve a team from 70–90 to 90–70. "In my heart, I don't feel we need Dawson," he said. He called the whole thing a circus, and said that Moss "wants to put on a dog and pony show at my expense." Accustomed to being the man in charge, Green was on the defensive. If he signed Dawson, he would compromise his stand against free agency; worse, he would do what he said he didn't want to do. If he didn't sign Dawson, there would be a public uproar and a hole in right field. And another factor was at work. The Cubs' attendance had declined slightly in 1986, and if they continued in their mediocrity — most of the forecasts placed them fourth in the National League East in 1987, ahead of only Montreal and Pittsburgh — they would forfeit all of the momentum that remained from 1984. The Cub rage would be over. And if that happened, the Tribune Company, owner of the Cubs, would of course have to reevaluate its executive personnel.

By the end of the week, Dawson was a Cub. Green was surprised that a player of such repute could be had for five hundred thousand dollars. For his part, Dawson was surprised he would be offered the lowest salary of any of the Chicago regulars, with the exception of Dunston, who had less than two years of major-league experience. But the contract did hold out the possibility of more money — one hundred fifty thousand dollars if Dawson made it through the All-Star game without going on the disabled list, and another fifty thousand if he made the All-Star team.

After the late start, Dawson had a good spring. He hit a

home run against the Brewers in Chandler and then two more against Seattle in Tempe. It was enough to provide Cub fans with the optimism they required to begin the season.

The Cubs were playing the Cardinals, which was dumb. There were 38,240 people at Wrigley Field, and there would have been that many if the Cubs had been playing the Bombay Bicycle Club on Opening Day. The Cardinals would sell out Wrigley Field on Christmas, but anyway, in the wisdom of the National League, it was Sutcliffe against John Tudor to start the 1987 season. Vince Coleman grounded out for the Cardinals, Ozzie Smith did the same, and a guy in the left-field bleachers announced he was headed downstairs for playoff tickets.

Sutcliffe worked out of the first, and then Bob Dernier, whose leadoff ability had declined to an unacceptable standard the previous two years, started the Cubs out with a single to left. This brought up the possibility of stealing a base against catcher Tony Peña, a former All-Star whom the Cardinals had acquired in a trade with Pittsburgh. "It's not a good idea to run on Peña," a Cub fan in the bleachers told his buddy. "I'm still pissed they got him." Ryne Sandberg, the teen-idol second baseman who had grown a mustache over the winter and shaved it after eighty-seven percent of people responding to a poll by the *Chicago Sun-Times* said they didn't like it (though he denied that was the reason), doubled. Then Dawson, batting for the first time as a Cub, hit a ground ball that was muffed by Tom Herr, the second baseman. Keith Moreland, an erstwhile outfielder who had been moved to third base for the season despite the skepticism of many who had watched the wide-legged Ron Cey for four years — a longtime Cub fan, Sara Davis, had expressed the prevailing sentiment one day during spring training when she said, "Moreland's a helluva nice guy and he'll do anything they ask him to do, but he's too fat for the job" — drove in a run with a fly ball, and after an inning the Cubs led 2–0. Vrdolyak was still in the game at that point, too.

He was also *at* the game, and if the mayoral vote had been taken inside Wrigley Field, Vrdolyak would have probably won in a walk, much in the manner that St. Louis eventually did. The Cook County Democratic Party chief referred to himself as the leader of the party's "white wing," and the Wrigley Field crowd was and traditionally is as white as any Yuppie or European precinct in Chicago. It was no coincidence that while Vrdolyak — who was running on the Solidarity Party ticket despite his Democratic position — and Republican candidate Donald Haider worked both the ballpark and the nearby taverns on election day, Washington was nowhere to be seen around Wrigley Field. It was an interesting coincidence, though, that the election and the first game fell on the same day. It meant, if nothing else, that Chicago was guaranteed at least one winner on April seventh.

By the third inning, though, it was becoming apparent that the Cubs would not be among that number. Sutcliffe, who had been handed the Opening Day assignment despite a miserable 1986 and a lackluster spring training, soon developed an acute disinclination to throw the ball over the plate. He walked five Cardinals in the third inning alone, and didn't even finish it. The Cardinals scored a run for every walk, and Kate and Mimi left for Murphy's Bleacher Bar across the street.

As the deficit lingered, the Cub fans, showing no effects from a long winter layoff, pulled out their old tricks. The first target, of course, was Sutcliffe. As the wealthy pitcher left, a red-faced middle-aged man standing behind the seats in right-center field and wearing one of the seventy-dollar satin Cub jackets (it was 46 degrees) screamed, "You're a bum, Sutcliffe! Take the money and run, you bum!" The same guy picked on Dawson moments later, when the new rightfielder came to bat. The previous time, batting with the bases loaded, Dawson had hit a massive drive to left that the wind blew foul, then popped up. "Dawson, you're a bum!" the man hollered. "Did you get a hit with the bases loaded? No! You're a bum! Welcome to Chicago!"

The fans in right field yelled at the St. Louis rightfielder,

Tito Landrum, and Landrum pointed to the scoreboard. Then they yelled at left field in the traditional Wrigley Field salutation. Right field: "Left field sucks!" Left field: "Right field sucks!" And so on. Inspired, the people on the Waveland Avenue (left field) rooftops took up the chant, their object of course being right field. Unappreciative of the support, the fans in the left-field bleachers turned and hollered at the roof people. "Scabs!" they called out.

Then Jerry Pritikin's plane flew over. Pritikin, a fifty-year-old superfan who called himself the Bleacher Preacher, had hired an airplane to carry the banner HARRY CARAY FOR PRESIDENT. It was a nice touch; Caray, the beloved announcer, was home in California recovering from a stroke. It was also expensive for a man without a job. "Sure, it costs," said Pritikin, "but I've got a reputation to uphold."

Pritikin had just moved back to Chicago from San Francisco, where he had worked as a self-employed photographer and publicist, and he intended to be at every Cubs home game in 1987. He made every game but one in 1984, after he won a lawsuit and used the money to spend that summer at Wrigley Field. This time, though, there was no job or settlement to fall back on. "I'm a professional fan," said Pritikin.

The manifestations of this were several. Pritikin wore a hat with a propeller on top and a T-shirt with BLEACHER PREACHER on the back. On the front of his shirt was the question, HOW DO YOU SPELL BELIEF?; and the answer, C-U-B-S. His self-appointed duty as the Bleacher Preacher was to save lost baseball souls who cheered for other teams, which he did by invoking the names of Bill Veeck, Sr., the father; Bill Veeck, Jr., the son; and Charlie Grimm, the Cubs' holy spirit. Occasionally, he brought to the games a voodoo doll depicting a particularly evil opponent and invited fans to stick pins in it. He made signs, gave out awards, and presented Cub decals to anybody who threw back a home-run hit by somebody on the other team.

What Pritikin did not do, though, was drink beer. In the bleachers, this distinguished him as much as the propeller on his head. In my naiveté, I had not understood the vested partnership that beer held in the bleachers. It was a firm of four: sun, people, beer, and ballgame. The pecking order was interchangeable, depending on the crowd, the weather, and the score.

On Opening Day, the crowd was large, the weather was chilly, and the score was 9–3. When the game ended, an older couple walked slowly down Sheffield Avenue. The man was wearing a Cub jacket over a Cub T-shirt from 1984, and on top of his head was a popcorn bucket turned upside down with the bottom torn out. Through the hole in the bottom were stacked beer cups too numerous to count.

Joe Mantegna et al. *

From *Bleacher Bums*

List of Characters

MELODY: an attractive and serious sun-worshipper.

GREG: a gentle young man in his 20's; blind from birth.

ZIG: a large man in his 50's. He is able to bellow and chew on a cigar simultaneously.

DECKER: a successful, energetic businessman, around 40 years old.

RICHIE: in his 20's. His personal habits and hygiene are disgusting.

MARVIN: a professional gambler, 30 or so.

CHEERLEADER: a hyper-active teenage fanatic.

ROSE: Zig's wife of 30 years and a closet Cub fan.

[*The year is 1977; it's a warm, sunny afternoon at beautiful Wrigley Field, and the Cubs are leading the Cards 5–3 behind ace Rick Reuschel. Here in the right field bleachers, the betting has been hot and heavy, with crusty, impulsive ZIG and earnest DECKER — a pair of die-hard Cub fans — losing a fair*

*A Nine-Inning Comedy conceived by Joe Mantegna and written by Roberta Custer, Richard Fire, Dennis Franz, Joe Mantegna, Josephine Paoletti, Carolyn Purdy-Gordon, Michael Saad, Keith Szarabajka, and Ian Williams under the direction of Stuart Gordon, with additional dialogue by Dennis Paoli.

amount of money to the slick, mercenary MARVIN, who always seems to win by betting against the Cubs. Unlike Marvin, sloppy nerd RICHIE is a Cub fan, but he also admires Marvin's gambling prowess, and has been trying to make the same bets as him. Meanwhile, an incredibly loud and annoying kid named CHEERLEADER keeps appearing on the scene to whoop it up for the Cubs and mercilessly taunt the Cards' right fielder, Mike Anderson. Blind, mild-mannered GREG has been listening to the game on his transistor radio, and gives a running commentary. He's also starting to make friends with sexy MELODY, who has come out more for the sun and relaxation than for the game itself.

The tension is mounting as Decker, reacting to Marvin's derision for making wimpy bets, wagers him $1,000 that the Cubs will win the game. The wicket is getting stickier for Zig, too, as his wife ROSE, tired of coping with Zig's constant gambling losses at Cub games, has showed up at the park and tracked him down. Now, as Zig makes a $30 bet with Marvin that the Cubs will score again, Rose cancels it out by making a $30 bet with Decker against the Cubs scoring.

Cubs coming up in the bottom of the eighth — play ball!]

ZIG: Rose, I'm askin' you as your husband. Please don't make this bet. Rose, I swear if you let me make this one bet by myself, I swear I won't make no more bets — today. That's the last one. Rose, I'm almost crying.

ROSE: That's not good enough, Herb.

ZIG: What do you mean?

ROSE: I mean I'll cancel my bet with Mr. Decker if you agree to give up gambling altogether. No more betting at the track, on the Bears, the Bulls, the Blackhawks —

ZIG: Let's not get stupid about the whole thing Rose.

ANNOUNCER: Pitching for St. Louis, #39, Al Hrabosky.

GREG: The Mad Hungarian!

ANNOUNCER: First batter for the Cubs, Ivan De Jesus.

ALL: Yay!

ZIG: De Jesus! Jesus! Come on Rose! This is De Jesus!

ROSE: I've had it, Herb. I'm sick and tired of not knowing if you're gonna come home with your pockets empty or what. I'm fed up with you walkin' out and leaving me for whatever game is in town.

ZIG: All right, Rose. You got me. You got my word of honor.

ROSE: Forever, Herb. For good. No more gambling.

ZIG: All right, Rose, you win. (*Strike one.*)

MARVIN: Strike, that's the way.

ROSE: Mr. Decker? Mr. Decker. I would like to cancel our bet. Would that be all right with you?

ZIG: What d'ya say, Deck?

DECKER: The whole family's into canceling bets. (*Strike — boo.*)

ZIG: Come on, Decker. Do the little lady here a favor, huh?

DECKER: For you, Rose — anything. (*Strike — awww!*)

RICHIE: Strike three! That was fast!

ZIG: Let's go, Ivan! Knock it outa the park!

MARVIN: He just struck out. Don't you ever watch the game?

GREG: Come on, Gene!

ROSE: I'm taking you at your word, Herb.

ZIG: Yeah. (*Yelling.*) Come on Cubs, let's score one here!

ROSE: How much you got riding on it, Herb?

ZIG: Thirty bucks. (*A hit.*)

DECKER: Look out! Not far enough.

CHEERLEADER: Drop it, Brock!

ALL: Awww!

ANNOUNCER: Ladies and gentlemen, batting for Bill Buckner, #1, Jose Cardenal!

CHEERLEADER: (*He passes out whistles as he talks.*) All right, this guy's real fast. We can do something for him. Take these whistles and blow them on every pitch. Then the outfielder can't hear the crack of the bat and he won't get a good jump on the ball.

MARVIN: Hey now, wait a minute!

CHEERLEADER: Come on, Jose! All the way! When I drop my arm!

MARVIN: (*To* RICHIE.) Don't blow that. (*All whistle except*

MARVIN *and* RICHIE. *A hit — fielder misjudges the ball and it gets trapped in the corner.*)

ZIG: That's hit!

MELODY: It's coming out here.

DECKER: It worked. It's in there.

CHEERLEADER: He lost it. He can't see it. It's rolling all the way to the wall.

MARVIN: It's over there, you rummy!

CHEERLEADER: Go! Go!

GREG: Cardenal's rounding second, he's on his way to third!

ROSE: Oh, oh, he found it.

DECKER: Fall down, you freak! (*He does.*)

MARVIN: Get up, you schmuck, and throw the ball.

ZIG: He's goin' for the plate!

RICHIE: Here comes the relay.

CHEERLEADER: An inside-the-park home run! (*Big cheer.*) We did it! (*Everyone goes nuts.*)

RICHIE: That wasn't fair!

CHEERLEADER: All's fair in love and baseball!

ZIG: We did that! We did that!

ALL: Hey! Hey!

ZIG: Go Cubs go! Marvin, you owe me. Look here, Deck! Look what I got in my hand from Marvin. Marvin just gave me something out of *his* pocket.

DECKER: You'll eat like a king tonight. The House of Sweden.

ROSE: Let me see, Herb. Let me count it.

ZIG: Thank you, Marvin.

ROSE: Ninety dollars!

ZIG: Three to one on thirty.

ROSE: I have ninety dollars!

ZIG: *We* have —

ROSE: Just let me hold it a second.

ZIG: Just put it in your wallet, Rose. Put it in your purse.

CHEERLEADER: Come on Bobby! (*Organ sounds.*)

ALL: Charge!

ROSE: Herb, I can get my hair fixed. I can have a facial and a manicure, both on the same day.

GREG: Show no mercy, Murcer!

ROSE: I can get the rug shampooed. We can get the drapes done.

ZIG: You can go to Sears and get all new stuff! Come on, Cubs, let's go!

ROSE: Oh, I don't think I ever put this much money in here before. Look how fat it is. (*A hit flyout.*)

ALL: Awww!

GREG: That's okay — we got another one. Ladies and gentlemen, moving into the top of the ninth inning, it's the St. Louis Cardinals three, the Chicago Cubs six. Just three more outs!

ANNOUNCER: Now playing first base for the Chicago Cubs, #26, Larry Biittner.

ALL: Yay!

ANNOUNCER: First batter for St. Louis, Gary Templeton.

ALL: Boo!

ZIG: Hey hon, I know I promised you no more bets. You see, I do have one other small bet. Now if you want me to cancel —

ROSE: What is the bet?

ZIG: It's a game bet with Marvin. A hundred bucks on the Cubs.

ROSE: You bet one hundred dollars on the Cubs?!

ZIG: I know —

ROSE: Herb, they're three runs ahead.

ZIG: Yeah —

ROSE: For God's sake, Herb, double the bet! Lay him odds!

DECKER: Come on, three up, three down!

ZIG: Hey, Marvin, Marvin! (*A hit — close play at First — he's safe.*)

ALL: Awww!

CHEERLEADER: Safe! He was out by three feet! That ump is blind!

GREG: Even I could see he was out.

MARVIN: Okay, we got a rally here.

DECKER: One hit ain't exactly a rally, Marvin.

ZIG: Hey Marv, I got a proposition for you. How about doublin' our bet — (*Pause.*)

MARVIN: Let's go, Cruz! Keep it alive.

ZIG: Not interested, huh? Ain't gonna take it. He knows when he's well off. We got him over a barrel, Rose. (*To MARVIN.*) We'll be thinkin' of you tonight over at the House of Sweden. (*A hit.*)

DECKER: Look out!

ALL: Booo! (MARVIN *applauds.*)

RICHIE: Okay! We got something going. Runners on first and second!

GREG: That's okay, now we go for the big double-O.

MELODY: Double what?

GREG: Double play.

CHEERLEADER: Hey, hey, what d'ya say, let's get a double play! (*Three times.*)

DECKER: Foul ball.

CHEERLEADER: Two men on. Two men on.

DECKER: How many outs?

RICHIE: None!

ROSE: We got faith.

MARVIN: Come on, Simmons. One swing of the bat can tie it up. (*Easy grounder to short — an error.*)

ALL: Yay — Awww!

DECKER: A perfect double play ball.

ZIG: Tailor made.

MELODY: But he dropped it.

MARVIN: That's your boy De Jesus. Easy play and he blows it.

RICHIE: Bases loaded.

CHEERLEADER: We gotta do something. The Cubs ain't playin' right. We gotta do something.

ZIG: What are you gonna do? Sit down.

CHEERLEADER: The Cards got the momentum. We gotta do something! Bobby, Jerry and Ivan, I'm coming! (*He tries to scramble over the wall onto the field. He is pulled back. He runs off, very upset.*) I gotta stop this game.

ZIG: There's somethin' wrong with that kid.

MARVIN: Hey Zig, you still want to double the bet? Six to three, bases loaded. Nobody out.

DECKER: Hey, they're takin' out Reuschel! (*Cheer for the departing pitcher.*) What did I tell ya? It's Sutter time.

ZIG: Hey, is Sutter comin' in? Is that Sutter?

ANNOUNCER: Ladies and gentlemen, now pitching for the Chicago Cubs, #42, Bruce Sutter. (*All cheer.*)

ZIG: We're goin' to a restaurant and a show tonight. Damn right we double that bet. That's money in the bank, Frank!

(ROSE *giggles. Organ plays "Plop, Plop, Fizz, Fizz, Oh What a Relief He Is." They sing along.*)

DECKER: Strike one! (*All cheer.*)

ZIG: He's got it today. They might as well throw in the towel right now.

ALL: Yay!

ZIG: That was his fork ball.

ROSE: It's really a split-fingered fast ball.

DECKER: Let's get out of this jam. Come on. Come on.

MELODY: Swing and a miss! (*Strike out.*)

ALL: Hey! Hey! Struck him out! The S.O.

RICHIE: That's only one out. The bases are still loaded.

ZIG: Don't you know who that is out there, you little putz? That's Bruce Sutter!

MARVIN: Let's go, let's go. (*All cheer.*)

ZIG: Where's the guy with the whistles now? We could use him.

DECKER: I can't believe he left. (*All cheer.*)

ZIG: Strike two! All right Brucie!

GREG: Six straight strikes. Six straight strikes!

ALL: Six straight strikes. Six straight strikes! Yay!

ZIG: He did it! (*All cheer.*)

DECKER: Two gone. Who's this — Anderson!

ALL: Booo!

MELODY: Hey you big dumb busher Anderson!

GREG: You got his number now, lady. (*Ball — all groan.*)

DECKER: That's okay. That's okay.

ZIG: They can't all be strikes.

ROSE: He just wants the people to get their money's worth.

ZIG: We're getting our money's worth. Right, Marvin?

DECKER: We need that kid now. He had that Anderson bugged.

ZIG: That's right. (*They look around. Strike. All cheer.*)

GREG: One and one.

DECKER: Slammin' the door on 'em.

ROSE: Bruce "The Savior" Sutter.

ZIG: Best pitcher in the National League. (*Ball — all groan.*)

GREG: That's okay, that's okay. Two and one.

ROSE: As long as he strikes him out, I don't care how he does it. (*Ball — all "AWWW!"*)

MELODY: Three and one. Don't walk him!

ROSE: No, no, that's all right honey. He does this all the time. He works best under pressure, see, so he builds the count on purpose.

ZIG: That's what I was gonna say! Hey, she knows. She knows.

DECKER: No walks, no walks, let's go. (*All cheer — strike.*)

ZIG: Full count. One more pitch and we can all get outa here.

DECKER: Hey, what's happening?

MARVIN: Why are they stoppin' the game?

ZIG: They're pointing at us.

ROSE: What are they looking at?

CHEERLEADER: (*Offstage.*) Sutter whooo! Sutter whooo! Sutter whooo! Sutter whooo!

MELODY: Now wait a minute. I hear that kid.

ROSE: Oh, my God.

DECKER: How'd that kid get up that scoreboard? (*Pandemonium breaks out.*)

ZIG: He's crazy.

MARVIN: He's gonna jump on the El.

ROSE: He's gonna fall and hurt himself.

MELODY: Uh oh, the guards are after him. Run! Now he's going up the flagpole!

MARVIN: Shoot him!

CHEERLEADER: We're number one! We're number one! We're number one!

ALL: We're number one! We're number one! We're number one!

RICHIE: They got him.

ALL: Awww!

DECKER: That's okay kid! (*Applauds.*) Now there was a Cubs' fan.

ZIG: Those young kids. They got too much energy. They should learn how to relax.

GREG: They're takin' their positions on the field again.

ZIG: One more Bruce, so we can go home, huh?

DECKER: Let's go, let's go, let's go! (*A hit — grand slam home run.* RICHIE *catches it.*)

RICHIE: I got it! I got it!

ALL: Booo!

RICHIE: (*Jumping up and down.*) We win! We did it! I caught the Grand Slam ball!

MELODY: Throw it back! Throw it back!

ALL: Throw it back! Throw it back!

RICHIE: You're crazy! We just won because of this. I'm not gonna throw it back. It's mine! Right, Marv? Hey, this is the guy! This is the guy! (*He hugs* MARVIN. MARVIN *pushes him away and throws his beer into* RICHIE'S *face.*)

MARVIN: You stupid moron! You little toad. You wanna buy me a beer? Fine! But keep your dirty hands off me. We won a couple bets, that doesn't make us buddies. Hey, nobody here can stand you. We laugh at you behind your back. We think you're a stupid fucking geek. An asshole. You know what I mean? (*To* ZIG.) Now we did double that bet, didn't we? (*Long pause —* ZIG *nods.*)

DECKER: Yeah. You can double ours too, Marvin. Make it two thousand.

RICHIE: And I want part of that. Even money on the Cubs.

MARVIN: All right. How's a thousand bucks sound? 500? 250?

RICHIE: Yeah.

MARVIN: 250? You sure you can cover it?

RICHIE: Yeah. Come on.

MARVIN: Okay, Richie, whatever you want to go for. (*A hit — easy out. All cheer.*)

GREG: And the side is out. But the damage has been done. Anderson's grand slam home run has put the Cards ahead seven to six going into the bottom of the ninth. Well, all we need is one to tie and two to win.

MELODY: All we need is two more runs.

ZIG: That's right. All it takes is two runs.

ROSE: And two is not so many.

MARVIN: Hey Decker, want to make a tie bet?

DECKER: I only bet on winners. (*He sits in his lucky seat.* RICHIE *sits next to him.*)

ANNOUNCER: First batter for the Cubs, Jerry Morales.

GREG: Come on, Jerry! Just get on!

ALL: We want a hit! (*Repeated three times. A hit — throw to First Base — easy out. All "AWWW!"*)

ZIG: That was a lucky catch.

DECKER: Nah, that Templeton's a good ball player. You gotta give him that.

MARVIN: One more, one more!

GREG: Come on, Steve! Let's pretend it's Christmas Eve!

ZIG: Hey, Marvin, will you sit down?

MELODY: That's a ball.

GREG: Good eye. Good eye, Steve. Look 'em over. Walk him!

DECKER: This is the last hope.

GREG: Come on, Mr. D. Ontiveros is gonna hit a homer. I know he is. (*A hit — cheer.*)

ZIG: That's hit! That one is hit!

GREG: Come on! Come on! (*Ball is caught — all "AWWW!"*)

MARVIN: And the Cubs lose again. All right! All right! The beginning of the end. Line up and pay the cashier. A good day! '69 revisited. The mighty Cubs. Hey, Ziggy, I'm real glad the little lady showed up today. If she hadn't doubled the bet —

ROSE: I know. Here's the money we won this afternoon, Herb. And here's the money I brought to the park today. What's left of it, and . . . I'm sorry. He's right; if I hadn't opened my big mouth and made you double the bet. . . .

ZIG: This little lady, I wouldn't trade her for nothing. I wouldn't trade her for De Jesus out there! This little lady you put that away. I tell you, Marvin, it's been a pleasure spendin' the day with ya. What is it, two C's? Here ya go. (*He pays* MARVIN.) Y'know Marvin, I got two champs. A champion team out there and I got a little champ right here.

ROSE: Oh, Herb.

ZIG: Come on, we're goin' over to the House of Sweden.

ROSE: Oh, no, no. That's all right. We can stop at the A&P. I can make cabbage rolls.

ZIG: Forget the A&P. Forget the cabbage rolls. We got a winning team right here, you and me. We're celebrating. And at least now I don't have to go home and tell you I dropped a couple of hundred. Greg, have a good day. See ya tomorrow.

ROSE: Yeah. We'll see ya tomorrow. (ZIG *is stunned at this. Then reconsiders.*)

ZIG: Yeah. We'll see ya tomorrow. (*They exit.*)

MARVIN: Decker, why do you do it? Why do you do it? You know what you are? You're a heart better. You keep bettin' with your heart, not your head. These guys are fold-up artists. Nobody ever went broke bettin' against the Cubs after the Fourth of July.

DECKER: Right, Marvin.

MARVIN: Hey, I used to be just like you, but I got burned one time too many. These guys are springtime wonders. I'm surprised at you.

DECKER: Yeah, I'm surprised at me too.

MARVIN: It's a town of masochists. They like to see themselves get beat. A bunch of losers.

DECKER: Losers, huh?

MARVIN: That's how I'm betting.

DECKER: (*Paying* MARVIN.) Here's the money, Marvin; don't spend it all in one place. There's still a few bets left this season.

MARVIN: Okay, Richie, 250 bucks. Cash on the line. You don't got it, right?

RICHIE: I don't have all of it with me.

MARVIN: Don't you know better than to make bets you can't cover?

RICHIE: Are you gonna be here at tomorrow's game?

MARVIN: Hey, hey, hey, I don't ever want to see you in this park again. If I do I'm gonna kick your ass. And I'm not bullshitting. Now get out of here. (RICHIE *starts to leave.*) And don't let me ever see you around here again.

DECKER: Hey, Marvin, is my marker good with you?

MARVIN: What are you —

DECKER: Is my marker any good? Yes or no.

MARVIN: I'll take your marker.

DECKER: (*Writes on his program and hands it to* MARVIN.) All right then, here you go. Well, what's the matter? You said you'd take it.

RICHIE: Decker, you mean . . .

DECKER: Yeah, yeah.

MARVIN: You gotta be the big man.

DECKER: What big man?

MARVIN: I mean you're gonna cover his bet?

DECKER: It's an investment, Marvin. I mean I'm a business man, right? He's my scorekeeper. My lucky scorekeeper. Very important.

MARVIN: Jesus, Decker . . .

DECKER: (*Shrugs.*) Be seein' ya, Greg. See ya around, Miss King. You stop back tomorrow. Next time they'll win one for you.

MARVIN: Hey, Richie, Richie, wait a minute. Look, I got a little excited there, you know. I mean, you're not supposed to make bets you can't cover. I just wanted — I wanted to make a point with ya. Ya know what I mean? Hell, other guys — ya go out in the real world and pull this kind of bullshit . . . Hey, wait a minute, wait a minute, you got the ball there, right? That grand slam ball?

RICHIE: Yeah.

MARVIN: I'm gonna give you fifty bucks for the ball. Hell, I'll give ya a hundred bucks. I'll give ya a hundred dollars for that ball. Yea, sure. That ball won me a lot of money and I just wanna show that there's no hard feelings. (RICHIE *starts toward* MARVIN, *holding out the ball. Then he turns and throws the ball back onto the field.*)

DECKER: See ya around, Marvin. Come on, Richie. (*They exit together.*)

MARVIN: (*To* MELODY.) Hey, honey, need a ride? (*He holds out a folded twenty-dollar bill.*)

MELODY: No, thanks.

MARVIN: Hey, lemme give you a ride home, Greg.

GREG: How much did you win today, Marv?

MARVIN: A lot of money, Greg.

GREG: Well, if you're smart tomorrow, you'll put all that money on the Cubs. 'Cause they're gonna win. You know why? 'Cause they're mad and when you're mad you get up and go, huh? As a matter of fact they're not only gonna win tomorrow but they're gonna take the rest of the series. Then they're gonna win three from Pittsburgh and then they're gonna take that series from Philadelphia. And those three Spanish ass-kickers are gonna keep on hittin' 300 ball. And Reuschel is gonna be a twenty-game winner and so's his brother. And Sutter, Marv, can you believe this? Sutter is not going to lose another game in relief. His Earned Run Average is gonna be .0000000001. And then at the end of the season they're gonna win the pennant. Oh, Marv, guess what? The Sox win too. Could you see that, Marv, could you see that? They'll call it the fifty cent series because that's how much it costs to go on the El between here and Comiskey. And they'll play the series and it'll go the full seven games. And they'll be in the seventh and it'll be all tied up in the twenty-third inning, 'cause it was a pitcher's duel all the way down — know what I mean? And then you know what's gonna happen? They're gonna bring in Ernie Banks out of retirement, and he's gonna hit a home run right into my lap and they win!! (*Big pause.*) And that's when you can give me a ride home, Marv.

MELODY: But now you're gonna walk me to the El.

GREG: But now I'm gonna walk Miss King to the El.

(GREG *and* MELODY *exit together, leaving* MARVIN *alone on stage.* MARVIN *shoves his wallet into his back pocket, looks around, picks up change thrown earlier to the* CHEER-LEADER, *sighs, and exits.*)

ANNOUNCER: Ladies and gentlemen, boys and girls, be here tomorrow for the second game in our series with St. Louis. If you're driving home, please drive carefully. Thank you and good night.

Gordon Edes

Funny How You Can
Date a Life with Baseball

Los Angeles Times, September 23, 1984

*By the shores of Lake Michigan, where the hawk wind blows so
cold, an old Cub fan lay dying, in his midnight hour the toll.*

*Around the bed his friends had all gathered, they knew his
time was short. And on his head they put a bright blue cap from
his all-time favorite sport.*

*He told them, "It's late, it's getting dark in here. I know it's
time to go.*

*"But before I leave the lineup, boys, there's one thing I'd like
to know.*

*"Do they still play the blues in Chicago when baseball season
rolls around?*

*"When the snow melts away, do the Cubbies still play in their
ivy-covered burial ground?"*

The song is called "A Dying Cub Fan's Last Request." It
was written by Steve Goodman, a Chicago folk singer, a lover
of baseball and a lifelong fan of the Chicago Cubs.

A year ago last winter, Goodman, touring with country
singer Johnny Cash, played a gig in a small auditorium at Fort
Pierce, Fla., near Dodgertown. A sportswriter attended the
concert, then went backstage and introduced himself to
Goodman. They talked baseball.

With a couple of days off, Goodman visited Dodgertown.

Team publicist Toby Zwikel, who once worked for UPI in Chicago, knew and admired Goodman's music. He took Goodman into the clubhouse and gave him a Dodger cap. Tommy Lasorda gave him an autographed ball and introduced him to the players.

At Holman Stadium in Vero Beach, they played one of Goodman's songs on the PA system. Goodman sat in the shade of the press box, joked with the writers, and made his predictions along with the rest. Everybody laughed about the Cubs.

Goodman also laughed about the illness he had that prompted the song. He joked about how chemotherapy had cost him his hair and how they had put a bulb in his head because they couldn't stick the needle in for any more spinal taps.

He was that kind of guy, a little guy who would laugh at anything. He once wrote an anti-nuclear song, "Watching Joey Glow."

Besides, leukemia was nothing new to him. He'd had it since 1969, the year the Cubs blew the pennant to the Amazin' Mets.

Funny how you can date your life with baseball.

"When I was a boy they were my pride and joy, but now they only bring fatigue.

"To the home of the brave, the land of the free and the doormat of the National League."

He told his friends, "You know the law of averages says anything will happen that can.

"But the last time the Cubs won a National League pennant was the year we dropped the bomb on Japan.

"The Cubs made me a criminal, led me down a wayward path,

"They stole my youth from me, that's the truth.

"I'd forsake my teachers to go sit in the bleachers in flagrant truancy,

"What do you expect when you raise up a young boy's hopes and then crush them like so many beer cups year after year after

year, so these hopes are just so much popcorn for the pigeons beneath the El tracks to eat."

For a while, the treatments seemed to help, just as they had when the leukemia went into remission in 1975. Goodman, who had moved to Seal Beach with his wife, Nancy, and their three daughters, recorded a couple of albums on his own label. He still toured some, even played Chicago a couple of times. He had season tickets for Angel games.

Once, before going into the hospital, he gave his copy of the *Baseball Abstract* to a sportswriter. He didn't fail to notice that the author, Bill James, said that if the Cubs were ever ripe for a miracle, this would be the year.

Goodman saw the Cubs play the Dodgers in early April and lose twice. The laughable, lovable Cubs. He expected little more from a team that once had an outfielder, Jose Cardenal, who couldn't play because his eyelids were stuck shut.

By the end of June, though, when they came in for four more games with the Dodgers, the Cubs were in a title race. Like many Chicago fans, Goodman suspected the Cubs were merely delaying their traditional June swoon, but still he was excited. The Dodgers invited him to sing the anthem.

Then, a few days before he was to sing, Goodman called a friend. Sorry, he said, but he had to go into the hospital. On Saturday, the day Goodman was to have sung, the Cubs beat the Dodgers and moved into first place, a game ahead of the Philadelphia Phillies.

"You know, I'll never see Wrigley Field anymore before my eternal rest, so if you have your pencils and scorecards ready, I'll read you my last request.

"Give me a doubleheader funeral in Wrigley Field on some sunny weekend day (no lights).

"Have the organist play the national anthem and a little na-na-na-na-hey-hey-hey goodbye.

"Make six bullpen pitchers carry my coffin, six grounds-keepers clear my path.

"Have the umpires bark me out at every base in all their holy wrath.

"It's a beautiful day for a funeral, Hey Ernie, let's play two.

*" . . . Give everybody two bags of peanuts and a Frosty Malt,
and I'll be ready to die."*

*. . . The dying man's friends told him to cut it out, stop it,
that's an awful shame.*

*He whispered, "Don't cry, we'll meet by and by in the
Heavenly Hall of Fame."*

*He said, "I've got season tickets to watch the Angels play
now, that's just what I'm going to do,*

*"But you, the living, you're stuck here with the Cubs, so it's
me who feels sorry for you. . . ."*

On Friday, the Cubs' magic number for winning the title in
the National League East was three.

On Friday, the playoffs were due to start at Wrigley Field
in 11 days. At the ballpark, they play a fight song called "Go
Cubs, Go." It was written by Steve Goodman.

On Friday morning, Steve Goodman died in a hospital in
Seattle. He was 36. He was a good man, a great fan.

Funny how you can date your life with baseball.

Mike Downey

In the End, the Cubs Are Still the Cubs

Los Angeles Times, October 10, 1989

A week ago, we all felt great. Now we've got 24 to 30 guys
who feel like they want to throw up.

— Rick Sutcliffe, Cub

Hey, I didn't give up a hit to Mario Mendoza, you know. I
gave up a hit to Will Clark.

— Mitch Williams, Cub

There's not a man among us who blames Andre Dawson or
Mitch Williams or myself or anybody else for us losing the
game. Will Clark won the game. San Francisco won the
game. We lost the game. The Chicago Cubs. All of us.

— Ryne Sandberg, Cub

I've had ups and I've had downs. This is a major down.

— Andre Dawson, Cub

I don't think Andre wants anybody to feel sorry for him.

— Mark Grace, Cub

Cub means always having to say you're sorry.

They wear the baby bear on their sleeve; you wear your
feelings there. They play; you pay. They live, they die; you
laugh, you cry. They win; you grin. They lose; you bruise.
They come from Chicago; you get the wind knocked out of

you. Either they leave you in stitches or coming apart at the seams.

For 113 years, they have been playing baseball profession- ally (well, playing professional baseball) and, to this day, they have never won a postseason game west of their city limits. Monday, they concluded a five-game series in which they outhit the San Francisco Giants in Games 2, 3, 4 and 5, and *still* won only once. Ladies and gentlemen, we give you the Chicago Cubs, a team from the National League that belongs in the National Lampoon.

Their clubhouse was so quiet, you could hear a pennant drop.

"Call it a crummy ending to a wonderful year," said Mark Grace, who may go down as the only man in baseball history to bat .647 in a playoff series and still be outperformed at his position. The only reason Americans today are not talking about the spectacle of Grace under pressure is because of this other guy, this Will Clark character, this dangerous man who clubbed the Cubs with his stick as cruelly as though they were baby seals.

Asked what would be the most memorable memory of his first National League championship series, Grace gave thought for only a few seconds.

"Will Clark," he said.

As *your* greatest memory?

"Well," Grace had to admit, "he kind of made himself tough to forget. You know?"

They were the stars of this show, these two first basemen. Together they cranked out 24 hits in five games, each man posting staggering slugging percentages of 1.100-plus, while fielding flawlessly. Herb Caen, a San Francisco columnist of note, summed things up perfectly for posterity, writing: "Will played with grace, and Grace played with will."

It finally got to the point where the Giants did everything in their power to avoid pitching to Grace, walking him delib- erately and daring Andre Dawson to do something about it, while the Cubs made the monumental mistake of walking so many Giants *un*intentionally that they had to pitch to Clark, who did do something about it.

Mitch Williams was assigned — forced — to pitch to Clark. NBC, for its final baseball telecast of a golden era, was rewarded with a stare-down between Chicago's finest relief pitcher and San Francisco's finest hitter with the score 1–1, the bases loaded and two out. How much more color could any peacock ask for?

By coincidence, at this very hour on another West Coast television channel, Williams' wife was talking to Joan Rivers on a previously taped talk show about the hardships and heartbreaks of being married to a ballplayer, of how when her husband was traded from Texas to Chicago, she "cried for two weeks." Little did Dee Williams know that when it comes to Cubs, you usually end up crying twice, coming and going.

Mitch Williams never was so sorry not to have to face Mario Mendoza in his life. He got two strikes on Clark but couldn't find a third. Clark's single through the box scored two runs, knocked Williams *from* the box after only one batter and left two lefties acquired from Texas, Williams and Steve Wilson, the pitching staff's guilty parties of Chicago's final two games.

Yet, don't feel sorry for them.

Feel sorry for Andre.

Don't take Grace's advice. Go right ahead, feel sorry for Andre Dawson. Feel sorry for this stand-up guy whose knees ache so badly that he can barely stand up. Feel sorry for this 35-year-old Ernie Banks-to-be who has never been to a World Series without a ticket. Feel sorry for this handsome, heroic figure who once put his signature on a blank contract and left the salary line blank, he wanted to play for the Cubs so badly. Feel sorry for him because he *played* so badly.

"I thought Dawson was gonna burn 'em," Grace said.

Instead, Dawson stranded 19 baserunners in five games. He hit .105. He struck out with the bases loaded for the final out of Game 4. He tapped out to the pitcher with two runners on base in the eighth inning of Game 5. He misplayed Clark's drive in right field that led to the Giants' game-tying run. Only a Cub could be the league's most valuable player (in 1987) when the club finishes in last place, then become their least valuable player after the club finishes in first place.

Dawson folded his arms, took a deep breath, took on all comers.

"It's not eating me up inside. It's not tearing me up inside," he said at his locker, assessing the damage. "But of course, it hurts. Of course, it hurts.

"I wasn't there when they needed me. I didn't do what I get paid to do. I was over-aggressive. A lot of things go through your mind, but all I can do is accept it. Maybe this will be the last chance I'll ever have. I'm trying to stay on an even keel because, well, what else can I do?"

You live with the Cubs, laugh with the Cubs, love the Cubs, loathe the Cubs, laugh *at* the Cubs. Whatever. You wait for next year. You wait for the year after that. You wait and you wait and you wait. What else can you do?

Jon Margolis

Would Chicago Be Losing Something If the Cubs Actually Won?

Chicago Tribune, October 5, 1989

Not, mind you, that anyone wants to lose.

Nor even that victory should not be followed by joy and rapture unconfined, as well as by beer and loud noises unconfined, as well as by parades, dancing in the streets, songs and poems and the feeling that there is a point to living, after all.

And yet . . . and yet . . . amidst all the high hopes and nervous optimism, here and there around town can be heard the suspicion that with joy comes . . . well, not regret, but complications.

Because if it really happens, if the Cubs win it all, not just the National League playoffs but the World Series, too, something would change. Part of what has sustained Chicago for decades — the sense of itself as tough, gritty, persistent but ultimately disappointed — would crumble.

"Chicago wouldn't understand its place in the world any longer," said Ron Berler, the Evanston teacher and writer who for years has followed the team's misfortunes and their effect on the city. "This would go to the very core of Chicago's self-conception."

No, Berler was not being entirely serious and, yes, it's just a few ballgames. Win or lose, a few days after the Series ends, people will go about their business, whether they are bemoaning another lost opportunity or savoring the success they feared might never come. And needless to say, there is a contrary opinion.

"I think there would be an improvement in the city's self-image," said William Erbe, a sociology professor at the University of Illinois at Chicago. "It could lead to all sorts of reminiscences about 1945," when, Erbe said, the city was more vigorous than it is now.

But if the Cubs become champions of the entire baseball world, still possible despite Wednesday's debacle, a piece of Chicago mythology would be destroyed. As evidence, consider this: Since June 11, Chicagoans have been filling most of the seats at the Organic Theatre to see a play called *Bleacher Bums,* and one reason the play is a hit is that its audience identifies with what its villain says near the end.

"These guys are fold-up artists," says Marvin after another Cub loss. "These guys are springtime wonders. They're heartbreakers." But it isn't just the team which Marvin is talking about. It's the city. "It's a town of masochists," he says. "They like to see themselves get beat. A bunch of losers." When he finishes, there is a palpable sense of self-recognition in the audience.

Winning the World Series could change that perception, as the folks behind *Bleacher Bums* are well aware. "We're discussing that right now," said producer Bob Perkins, when asked if there would have to be major changes in the scripts. "It's the subject of some debate."

It isn't that the Cubs and Chicagoans are "lovable losers." No, it's more complicated than that. The New York Mets, years before they became hateable winners, were lovable losers.

The Cubs represent something else, as illustrated in *Bleacher Bums* by the reply to Marvin from Greg, the loyal Cub fan. "Tomorrow, they're gonna win," he says, ever hopeful. And then he spins a fantasy of the Cubs winning the division, the pennant and the seventh game of the World Series on a ninth-inning home run by Ernie Banks, brought out of retirement for the occasion.

Chicago's sense of itself as symbolized by the last 80 frustrating years of its most revered institution — for that is what the Cubs are — is not a city of lovable losers but a city of dreamers in the face of impending doom, of people who hope for much even if they expect little, and who keep trying no matter how often they fail and no matter how ridiculous they may seem. Witness the chants of "Let's go Cubs," at the start of the bottom of the ninth inning Wednesday night despite the Giants' 11–3 lead.

There is a certain amount of reality behind that image. Because it kept trying, Chicago revived after the great fire, after the depression and after the tumult of 1968, which so badly tarnished its reputation. It is reviving now after the loss of its industrial economic base and its recent governmental zaniness.

Not that this tenacity makes Chicago unique. Other locales tell similar tales. Even the current enemy, San Francisco, battled back from the earthquake that nearly destroyed it in 1906. But San Francisco's sense of itself is haughty, not gritty. Besides, the Giants never have waited so long, or so often come so close, only to fail at the end.

Nobody has, which is why there is no way to measure what success would do to Chicago. The Brooklyn Dodgers finally won their World Series in 1955. Two years later, they were gone. Anyway, Brooklyn was not a city, only part of one.

The second longest wait is also Chicago's. The White Sox have not won a World Series since 1917. The Boston Red Sox won for the last time a year later, and just three years ago, they came within a pitch of the world championship. Red Sox fan Luke Salisbury, in his book *The Answer Is Baseball*, described the divided emotional state that may become familiar to Chicagoans this month:

"I, like many lifelong Sox fans, waited for what should have been the last out, and wondered what I'd do if they won. I thought I'd have to change my philosophy of life. The world wouldn't be the same. I have always known the Red Sox to lose big games, and I am fated to root for them. . . . But I also knew that if they won, they'd be just another team rather than an infuriating emblem of my psyche. "Don't think I didn't want them to win. I'd gladly trade my sense of the universe for the world championship. I just didn't know what I'd do. Weep? Repent? Vote Republican?"

The only other comparable case is the Mets, who remained lovable after their first improbable victory in 1969, but whose recent arrogance has annoyed even their own fans. But the Mets are in New York, which exudes arrogance. Chicago is not arrogant, at least not collectively. Individually, Chicagoans can be arrogant, even blunt. Oh, why euphemize? This can be a mean town. But it is just a bit too unsure of itself to be arrogant.

In fact, what Chicago has done, with the help of the Cubs, is to convert its inferiority complex into a strength. It always has been a bit less sophisticated or fashionable than some other cities — not just New York and Los Angeles, but also Minneapolis and Denver — so it has gloried in its artlessness.

And it has gloried in the Cubs' frustration. Even as the team headed toward a division championship, peddlers outside the ballpark were hawking T-shirts proclaiming "Ten Lies Told in Wrigley Field" — among them, "August is our month," a one-line parody about the Cub propensity to fall apart late in the season.

In addition to everything else, then, the Cubs and their failures have performed the absolutely necessary function of helping Chicagoans laugh at themselves. If they win, they may not be able to provide that service for a while.

Not to worry. Something will.

Epilogue

"World Champion Chicago Cubs."

No, it's not an oxymoron. As a matter of fact, it has a nice ring to it. What's more, I'm going to state right now, flat-out, that the Cubs are definitely going to win the World Series within the next five years.

How can I be so sure? Well, for one thing, the laws of probability weigh heavily in our favor. Consider this: there are six teams in the NL East, so each team should win the division, on the average, once every six years. So, assuming a 50% success rate in the playoffs — another long-term statistical probability — any given NL East team will win the pennant once every 12 years. The Cubs haven't won the pennant since '45, so the statistical likelihood is that between now and 1995 they will accumulate 4.167 NL flags. Thus, again assuming a 50% success rate in the Series, the Cubs will win not one, but two World Championships within five years! We're looking at a dynasty here.

Beyond the immutability of the numbers, there's this: the Cubs now have night ball, an ownership committed to winning, and the devotion and prayers of millions all over the hemisphere — not to mention the most promising crop of young players we've seen in a long time.

In '84 the Cubs proved that they could be winners. In '89 they proved that '84 wasn't a fluke. No question now: after

39 years in Purgatory, we're finally starting to get on a roll here. There's a tiny but unmistakable voice in the breeze wafting across Lake Michigan, through the caverns of Wrigley Field and into the collective inner ear of Cub fans everywhere, whispering, "Hold onto your hats, friends, because 'World Champion Chicago Cubs' is getting ready to happen."

Any year now.